Oh My God
You Are Really REAL

True Stories of When God Shows Up!

J. K. Sanchez
Along with 20 additional authors

All scripture quotations are taken from The ESV Bible (The Holy Bible, English Standard Version).

Scripture quotations are from The ESV Bible (The Holy Bible, English Standard Version®), copyright © 2001 by Crossway, a publishing ministry of Good News Publishers. Used by permission. All rights reserved.

Oh My God You Are Really REAL: True Stories of When God Shows Up
ISBN -13: 978-0692055694
ISBN – 10: 069205569X

Copyright © 2018 by J. K. Sanchez.
Published by: Button Lane Books Spanaway, WA 98387
Contact: www.jksanchez.com or jksanchez.author@gmail.com

Cover Artwork by: Antonia Frye
Cover Design by: J.K.Sanchez, Antonia Frye and ButtonLaneBooks

Printed in the United States of America. All rights reserved under International Copyright Law. Contents and/or cover may not be reproduced in whole or in part in any form without the express written consent of the Author.

Endorsements

"If you are looking for encouragement and inspiration that will revive your faith in God's supernatural abilities to perform the miraculous, *Oh My God You are Really Real*, provides just that! Written by several authors as a compilation of faith-building stories, this book reveals their unique journey in discovering God's faithfulness, provision, healing and love. You will be able to relate to many of the emotions, adventures and life experiences of the writers. As you put yourself in their shoes, you will be awakened to a greater understanding of God's unfailing love for each of us! This book will make your heart smile again!"

Ceitci Demirkova
Founder & CEO of "Changing a Generation".
Best-Selling and Award-Winning Author of *Motivated by the Impossible*
www.ceitci.org
www.invisiblementors.com

"A book of heavenly surprises. JK Sanchez has deftly gathered tales of unexpected help in times of distress, financial gifts in times of need, and the perfect friendship in times of loneliness. These stories will bolster your faith as you see God's mysterious hand at work in our lives."

 Peggy Frezon, author of *Faithfully Yours, The Amazing Bond Between Us and the Animals We Love*
www.peggyfrezon.com

Dedication

To those who desire to find, experience and walk in a new life with Jesus Christ.
He is a very REAL God who is faithful and good all the time.

To those whose stories fill these pages with truth of His goodness.

To those whose stories are yet to be written, as they encounter a God who is really REAL!

And above all:

To my God and Savior Jesus Christ!
UNTO YOU BE ALL THE GLORY!

Table of Contents
Provision

An Unassuming Trespasser	1
A Cow Directed by Heaven	9
20's from Heaven	12
Embers of Hope	16
Always on Time	23
A Day of Miraculous Multiplication	27
A Roller-Coaster of Divine Provision	33

Healing

"Call the Doctor – She Can See!"	39
Riding with the Wind	43
A Birthday Surprise from Jesus	47

Trust

Unrelenting Waves of Trust	59
God's Little House	68
Do I Trust God or Man?	73

Protection

His Reinforced Shelter	87
A Phantom Train	93

Intermission 95

Forgiveness

Out of the Ashes – Forgiveness Rises	99
A Road to Murder	105
A Choice to Forgive	114

Love

Two Love-hungry Hearts	121
Love Found in the Desert	127

Faith

Talk to Him like He is Real?	133
A Surprise Passenger	138
Faith is All You Have	141

Wisdom

"Here I am, Send Me!"	149
Road-trip of Rain and Revelations	157
Nail-Polish Wisdom	168

Contributing Authors, Editors and Artists	175
Endnotes	190

Acknowledgments

This book would never have come to life without an amazing group of writers who believed in, experienced and stepped forward to share the reality of a REAL God who personally showed up in their lives and transformed them. These stories, thought to be complete prior to this book, soon found renewed transforming power as many of the authors began the writing process. I am thankful, humbled and honored to have been a part of this project with each of you.

**Zelda Croskey, Makalai Michaels,
Veronica Erickson,
Linda Handschue, Lorena Hartzog,
Donna Jackson, Mark Johnson,
Patty Johnson,
Melissa Lee, Marilyn Love, Randy Love,
C. Marie,
Shellia Reed, Dennis Sanchez,
Bonnie Simmons, Nicholas Smurro,
Christine Vanderhoff, Dustie Verwers,
Stacy Wind and Kasey Zeigler**

Writing, rewriting, editing, editing, editing and rewriting, rewriting and rewriting - over the past year my unfathomable gratitude is to my amazing daughter-in-law, **Amber Sanchez** and my sister, **Donna Jackson** - your editing skills, dedication to the task and patience have been Herculean. Thank you for believing in and working diligently with me to bring a clear and concise group of stories to publication.

A huge thank you to my granddaughter, **Antonia Frye**! Your artistic talent, eye for detail and way-beyond-your-age maturity have thrilled my heart. Working with you to accomplish this book has been a great treasure to me.

With great appreciation, I am thankful for an untold number of prayer warriors - their time and prayers have prepared the way - your love and sacrifice has been felt every step of the way.

The list of those who have been instrumental in the accomplishment of this book has grown to include so many I am unable to list all of you. However, to a few of those whose support has been invaluable and made this book possible, I must say a huge thank you to you.

Joy Cornelius – Thank you for being my constant cheer-leader and friend.

Myra Pierce - Your prayers have gone before the throne and have kept me going. Thank you!

Pastors Bob Clark & Jim Sheen - Thank you for your encouragement, support and willingness to participate with perfectly concise words in just the right places.

Pastor Lorelei Sheen - Thank you first for being you and for being my friend! Your encouragement, honest direction, confidence building presence and willingness to give me a push in the right direction has been a wonderful unexpected gift.

Ceitci Demirkova and Peggy Frezon - Your willingness to set aside the "business" mentality and reach out to encourage and help a newbie author with her way-too-big-for-her project has been refreshing as well as humbling. Thank you for your encouraging words, direction, help and friendship.

Introduction

Inspirational true stories ignite hope in all of us. They stir us to believe in a creator who loves. A God who is good and shows us in ways that explode unexpectedly right before us. At those times, we are made acutely aware of HIS love, HIS goodness, HIS presence, and HIS reality.

True inspirational stories come from you and me; everyday people living everyday lives. Some are miraculous and ALL are the intimate hand of a loving God.

These stories can be as simple as finding scraps of wood to keep your home warm. An unknown person stopping to offer cash for a broken-down old car - just when you desperately needed to buy groceries, or thrift store shopping for a new job with no funds, only to find money in that used jacket. Then there are the stories we think of as the "big" ones.

Just a few of those "big" ones might be - a stroke victim miraculously seeing after permanent blindness was diagnosed; permanent spine damage instantly healed or the ability to forgive deep physical and emotional betrayal. Each of these stories will change lives. They affect those involved, those that surround them and those that hear their stories.

True stories open your eyes to see a God who is REAL! Once eyes are opened to believe, it is very hard to unsee Him. Belief begins to emerge and suddenly the reality of our Lord Jesus is standing before you - asking you to accept who He is.

Step into the pages of this book expecting to see a GOOD God – one who heals, protects, provides, speaks and transforms everyday people. Allow these true stories to encourage, bring hope and spark belief within your heart. Watch as your encounter with Jesus takes on a REAL aha moment of transformation in your life.

As you become conscious of Him, your perspective will forever be changed – His love, His presence, and His reality will become the forefront of your existence and suddenly from deep within you, you too will say, "Oh – My – God – YOU are really REAL."

"Encountering Jesus leads to a real moment of real transformation. He's real! He's not just a story to be believed, nor a philosophical truth to buy into. When you meet Him; you meet His goodness. You discover who you were truly meant to be because you're walking with Him. Let this testimony rise up in your heart: God is good!
I am loved!
And my life is in His hands!
Today, press into a fresh knowledge of His real-life mercies until you are changed. Celebrate what He has done for you. Know that He has prepared a way for you to possess life. As you walk with Him, make it real, and then you will find the transformation you've been looking for."[1]

"Pastor Jim Sheen – Zion's River – Tacoma, Wa."

<u>"Go home to your friends and tell them how much the Lord has done for you, and how he has had mercy on you."</u>
(Mark 5:19)

Provision

Philippians 4:19
And my God will supply every need of yours according to his riches in glory in Christ Jesus.

"His supply is according to His riches. Where are they found? In Christ Jesus. Make Christ your hiding place in the famine... and your supply will be abundant."[1]

Pastor Bob Clark – Crossover Ministries – Parkland, Wa.

An Unassuming Trespasser
By J. K. Sanchez

"How am I going to feed you?" This thought swirling unbidden through my mind as I poured my daughter her afternoon bottle, with the apprehension of no money and still a week until payday blatantly glaring over my shoulder. The reality of our problem brought increasing anxiety in my heart as each day moved forward. With a silent prayer, I pushed those thoughts away.

"It's just a week away, it'll be fine." I spoke aloud, to myself, as my mind - struggling with faith, tried to close the lid of concern. The nibbling doubt oozed out all afternoon and joined me as I crawled into bed with my husband that night. The calendar marching forward with no answers. Each day the milk disappearing and the cupboards echoing from emptiness. My thoughts of stretching milk with a little water began to seem like a "no-brainer."

Several days later, my one-year-old early-morning alarm clock sounded, just as every other day. My sweet daughter, Amber, happily jabbering in the other room let me know of her desire to be released from her crib entrapment. Her rumbling tummy now required Mommy's attention.

I became acutely aware of my situation as I opened the refrigerator. Filling her bottle from the milk jug, I began trying to guess how many bottles were left in this quickly-disappearing gallon.

As a young military wife and mother, the dates on the calendar that we circled in red always seemed very far apart. This time the reality of an empty checkbook, cupboards, and refrigerator drew me to the depths of fear.

"How am I going to feed you tomorrow honey?" The question that began ruminating in my mind several days ago, now was resurfacing with a fervency that increased the already heavy heart I was carrying.

As the morning progressed the cloud over my mind grew stifling. My normal morning ritual of playtime with my daughter had been stolen as my eyes focused on my failure to "fix" this problem.

For several days, I had looked around for items to sell or for some way to get a little money for just another gallon of milk. But now as the milk disappeared, that circle on the calendar seemed to move further away. "Fixing it" was way beyond my grasp.

As morning naptime approached, I trudged through the house laying Amber down with her bottle – this time her milk being weakened with water. Now alone, my heaviness overtook me. Tears ran and frustration spewed as I became undone before God.

My toddler-stage faith in Jesus was being shaken to its very foundation. *He's the provider, He's my father* rang in my ears, though doubt was overtaking my heart as reality was standing before me.

I cried, I prayed, I begged, I yelled – but nothing inside my heart changed. An hour or so later, I came to a place on my knees of giving up. There in the center of the kitchen floor all my emotions were spent, and I was empty! I stood up and began a very real and true conversation – a rant really – at God. I emphatically said, "God – you said you love me! You said you're my Father! You said you answer my cries!

You said you provide! HELP us! There is NOWHERE for it to come from, but I believe you know what I don't. Please fix this – we desperately need food!" My fuming now complete, but tears continued to flow down my face as I began to accept the fact that I was not in control anymore. Though exhausted from a morning of intense emotion, I got up from the floor, washed the tears away and robotically moved about accomplishing those necessary chores that can only be done while my toddler was sleeping.

As I began to simmer beans on the stove – my only option for dinner – I realized the heaviness seemed to have lifted. Even if it was only for a short time, I was relieved that it was off my mind.

Inevitably my outburst and struggle with emotions had to be set aside as giggles began to erupt from the back room. Naptime was complete, and Amber was up and ready to play with more than the stuffed bunny in her crib. I was soon distracted as I became aware of the music streaming in from the living room. Here I found Amber, with my dishtowel in hand, tiptoe dancing and swirling around my feet as I cooked. Her joy and innocence were contagious.

Quickly we were singing and dancing around on the same floor that I had recently been crying and kneeling on. Suddenly this afternoon felt a hundred miles away from my intense morning. Though nothing had changed, the ominous burden had somehow been lifted during the morning's struggle.

Unexpectedly there was a knock at the back door. Since our little rental house was securely backed up against a secluded alley, my first response was one of surprise. *That's strange,* I thought, *wrong time for Dennis to be home.* I headed to the door expecting to see my husband home early without his key. But to my consternation, there stood a clean-cut middle-aged man gazing at me through the glass in the door.

As I look back, I should have been filled with fear, but instead my thoughts were more like: *What the heck? What is he doing in the alley? And why has he entered through my back gate? And even more concerning, who is this man standing at my back door?* But never once in that very rapid-fire exchange in my mind did I entertain fear.

I tentatively opened the door and greeted the stranger. The question from his mouth sent a shockwave through every cell of my being.

After that first question, I heard nothing else, for the blood that had rushed to my ears was now pounding fiercely through my head. I thought for sure I was going to faint and hit this same kitchen floor yet again today; my ears rang and the pressure in my head was as if I had sunk into deep water.

"Would you like to sell that old car?" this unassuming trespasser asked. His question reverberating in my spirit as if a trumpet had been sounded in the room. My mind raced, *Old car? What old car?* Then with surprise I quickly realized he meant the beat up, not working, piece of junk that we just couldn't afford to have hauled away that was sitting by the garage in the alley. Trying to be nonchalant, I stammered, "I'm sure my husband would be willing to let it go, but it's not running right now." My heart was screaming – *YES, YES, YES!!!*

"It's just for parts, so that's just fine. How is $300?" He questioned with a smile.

I nodded because no words could possibly come from my mouth since I wasn't even sure I was breathing.

My mind reeled with what was happening in front of me as several things quickly blew through the spinning cobwebs in my mind: *I'm going to throw up. This must be a dream. These things don't just happen!*

As he handed me the cash, I willed my hand to reach out and take it – afraid that this obvious apparition would dissolve. I stood transfixed as I watched him walk away, return quickly with a tow truck, attach it and drive away with that piece of junk (which to my rejoicing heart was now solid gold).

As the last rattle of the truck disappeared, I was still standing at the back door gripping that $300 in my trembling hand. Then my legs folded under me and my knees hit the floor for the second time that day. Tears ran again, but this time in awe of the obvious hand of God in answering my earlier prayer.

My faith exploded that day! I understood to the core of my being that my God is a good Father – one who loves me, who hears me, who answers me and who *does* provide for me.

Now, nearly 40 years later, the faith that was birthed in me that day has been my unshakable foundation and has shaped who I am.

The understanding of the power of our prayers and the listening ear of "Abba Father" has grown in me through many of life's daily struggles and has always brought me back to a place of walking in His presence with a submitted heart that is willing to kneel before a loving father.

His unfailing love, presence, and faithful provision is always available to us. When we don't understand, when things don't look like they are going right, and even when we get angry with Him, He still has it all under control – and if we can rest in that, we will see His hand in every situation.

I have learned that He often shows his power at the last minute and through unexpected willing strangers or those angels unaware. My memories of that day often make me wonder if I will someday meet this angel – this unassuming trespasser – in the throne room of heaven.

(Previously published – *Keeper of the Faith* 2016 Love INC Publishing)

A Cow Directed by Heaven
By Mark Johnson

A hot summer sun beat down as we pulled a little travel trailer onto the land. My wife and I had just purchased five acres of raw land east of Yelm, WA. Our intent was to build a house, a workshop, a barn, and fences, in that order. Things didn't happen quite like I planned them.

My wife quickly went to work as a schoolteacher and I took a union job for a year. At the end of that year I came home to build our little place. The undertaking was daunting, but I began by clearing out the property with the idea of establishing fence lines to build the house and barns and all that was needed.

I labored for two weeks digging postholes, pounding posts, stretching wire, and building gates. In the end, I had perimeters established and the place completely fenced.

The whole time I worked, my thoughts ran to where to buy cows. Having had three years of agriculture studies in high school and raising calves, my intent was to have beef cows in a pasture. But being years out of touch I just wasn't sure where to go, how to buy, or what to buy to get started again. God heard my mental queries as I worked, and He soon showed me how He attends to our every need.

As I hung the last three-foot man gate, which completed my several-week-long fence project, I heard a serious disturbance in the surrounding woods. Bellowing for all she was worth; a purebred registered Angus cow came crashing through the woods! In my shock, I simply opened the man gate and that cow ran through as if directed by heaven.

All I knew about this cow in my pasture was that she was in heat and her brisket tag read #65. Finally, after two weeks of searching, we found her owner.

The man had bought her for slaughter, as she had been deemed a "dry cow" – incapable of reproducing. Had she been able to reproduce, her assessed value at that time could have been $1200 – so without hesitation I accepted the man's offer and bought the cow for $250.

Ms. Cow, as we called her, quickly settled into her new home. Believing she could be capable of reproducing, and being a man of prayer, I called for her to be artificially inseminated. Nine months later we were blessed with a magnificent calf – crossbred of Belgian Blue and Black Angus.

Ms. Cow, aka #65, went on to bless us over the years with eight more calves.

God not only presented us with this cow before we could even ask, but He gave us a cow of an exceedingly gentle and faithful nature, always affectionate and attentive toward us and her calves.

The day she rambled through the woods and into our newly readied pasture was a simple reminder to me of how real God is and that He hears our prayers. Not only does He provide, but He also provides the very best.

20s from Heaven
By Donna Jackson

"I got the job!" I shouted with excitement. What an answer to prayer! Our financial struggle had become overwhelming and my return to the workforce was the only solution. The kids now were old enough to handle mom going off to a job. The offer to return to the bank where I had worked 15 years earlier was a bonus in every way.

My excitement permeated the whole house; the kids and Mike were all behind me. Then out of my daughter's mouth came a question that stumped me, "What are you going to wear mom?"

This was a simple question from a teenage girl, but to me it felt like a hammer had just shattered my excitement. I had been a stay-at-home mom for so many years I no longer had any business attire to begin work – jeans, sweatpants, shorts, and T-shirts were all that filled my closet.

I plastered my smile back on my face and responded with as much faith as I could, "I don't know yet, I guess it will be a surprise."

I called my long-time friend and "to-be" supervisor, pouring out my concern. I had no answer and was ready to throw in the towel on this job and resign to our financial plight. In the middle of our conversation, Jo suggested, "How about checking a thrift store for business jackets? They are bound to have a few nice ones for just a few dollars."

"Well, I guess before I quit even before I start, I should give that a try." I responded. Armed with my single $20.00 bill, a prayer to find something for that small amount, and an armload of doubt and discouragement, I walked into the thrift store to scour through mountains of old clothes.

To my amazement, I found racks of business attire waiting just for me! They were beautiful, and just what I needed. I approached the register with a pounding heart, concerned that some of my choices would need to be returned due to lack of money. But to my great relief, my $20.00 bill covered them all, even the tax!

I walked out with an armload of business attire and restored hope in starting a new job with purpose.

I was filled with faith – I knew God had heard my prayers. He had provided the job and knew my concern over something we normally take for granted: our clothes. But what happened next was so overwhelming that even today – many years later – I have to smile and say, "WOW GOD, YOU LOVE ME!"

Upon returning home with my bags of clothes, I began trying them on to show my husband what I found. Suddenly, I stood stock still, as I reached into the pocket of one of the jackets.

"There is something in here," I announced to Mike, "and it feels like money." Pulling out what my fingers touched, I carefully unfolded two $20 bills. The reality hit me: God not only answered my prayer of finding the necessary clothes for my $20.00 limit, *but He had returned it and doubled it.*

And if that wasn't enough, the next day I went into my backyard to water my flowers and there, crumpled up in the far back corner, was *another $20 bill!* God is good and gives us sweet surprises. He often speaks loudly to us about how much He loves us in unexpected ways.

When I had hesitantly responded to my daughter, "I don't know, I guess it will be a surprise." I never knew what a surprise He had waiting as He showed me His love and abundance, or that I would be returning to work dressed by my Heavenly Father's hand.

Embers of Hope
By Marilyn Love

BAM! The front door slammed shut in my face. Tears rolled down my cheeks as I watched my husband drive down our road to the highway. "Gone. He's really gone this time," my despondent heart whispers.

My gut hurts, my head is pounding, my eyes are puffed up as tears are cascading down my cheeks like a downpour of winter rain. "Oh my God! Now what do I do? I have no job, no bankroll to fall back on, no money tucked away for a time such as this. I have nothing! All I have is heartache, tears and shame – lots and lots of shame," my mind quickly firing out thoughts heavenward.

Here I found myself sitting on my expensive sofa, looking out onto the bay from our lovely home perched on the cliff, broken-hearted and empty.

As my sobs turned inward, I began pondering my life with its twists and turns. That previous life now was piled at my feet, smoldering. All my dreams had gone up in smoke with the slamming of the front door.

This huge home with its panoramic view of the glistening bay was our dream home. These wrap-around windows brought me such joy: watching eagles soar, seeing freighters brought into the bay with tug boats on each side, watching the draw bridges rise high in the sky to allow them to slip into their berths as the unloading and reloading to and from faraway destinations commenced. All of that – and so much that could have been – all – now dissolving before my eyes.

Fears and questions spun through my mind.

"Unknown, so much right now is unknown. Will he come home? Did I want him back home?" the questions circled as the fears began to permeate.

"He has snapped. I know he will never come back and I really don't think I want him back – I'm terrified of him.", my mind continued to spin.

"He makes me feel unworthy, stupid, shameful, unlovable." My heavy thoughts settling in.

Yet here I sit, trembling and scared. I have nothing but a roof over my head.

The numbness begins to wear off and the late evening hour makes me feel the coldness of the house. More disconcerting thoughts surface, "This nearly 4,000-square-foot home is a lot of space and to heat it costs a fortune. Money that I don't have." Through more tears, my self-pity begins to slide to the side and my faith begins to rise as I whispered, "Lord, I have two wonderful fireplaces in this huge house. The front room fireplace has a blower that could heat this whole floor. I have big pieces of dried wood ready to ignite, but I have no kindling to build that fire. Lord, you are now my husband. Please bring me some kindling so I can heat this home."

A few days later and still no kindling had arrived. Deciding to take a drive – I was on the lookout for what might work. I began nearing an intersection as I drove down the port road. Suddenly, I heard a soft internal voice gently say, "Turn left at this light and stop only when I tell you to." So, I did.

As I approached Alexander Street, I heard a direct command, "Pull over onto the corner of that lot, park your car and get out." Once again, I did as I had been told.

Getting out and looking around on the ground, the only thing I saw was eight little pieces of wood that were used for door trim.

As much as I wanted to be excited and feel some relief regarding my cold-house status, these few pieces weren't much help. Mumbling my disappointment to myself, I picked up those wood pieces, pretending to be grateful. Sarcastically, I found myself showing my attitude in prayer as I whimpered, "Really, God? Really?"

In the midst of my "poor me" moment, I became aware of a voice yelling at me. Turning toward the voice, I was surprised to see I was standing and holding my tiny pieces of wood in a large lumber company parking lot.

"Hey Lady, just what do you think you're doing?" screamed an angry voice as he approached me with his forklift. I burst into tears and then quickly shifted to sobbing. With a heaving chest, I began telling this young guy my story. Shame held its grip on me and any trace of self-esteem had vanished.

I told him God had directed me to this very spot to get some kindling so I could heat my home, and that these eight pieces of wood were going to light my big logs into a warm fire.

I sounded like a crazy woman. This tattooed, scruffy-looking kid judgmentally replied, "Your husband was a fool to leave you alone and cold."

In the same breath, he let me know he didn't believe in God anymore, but that he did believe he could help me.

He announced, "See that sliding gate over there? Back your car up to that gate. I'm going to spill a whole dumpster of fresh kindling just for you!"

He drove his big forklift off, leaving me standing stunned and in tears.

Wiping my flowing tears, I shot up a faith-filled prayer, "Oh Lord, forgive me for doubting you, for being more than a quart low on faith, for throwing a tantrum over eight little pieces of trim wood, for walking in my flesh instead of in your Spirit. Oh, forgive me."

BAM! There piled next to my car was more wood than I ever thought I'd see.

My new friend hopped off his forklift and began loading my car. He barked out, "Where are your work gloves?" Mumbling an apology that I had none, he smiled as he realized I was pretty helpless. He continued loading my car, while I wept with joy. He was my angel! Introducing himself as he continued poking in the last possible piece of wood.

Upon completing the loading, he confidently explained, "Lady, when you start to run out of wood, you drive down here, back your car up to the gate and holler out my name. I'll give you more wood than you dreamed possible."

Believing in his offer I made many trips, and just as he had promised, he provided.

With each trip to get more wood, I consistently told him more about Jesus and how He was helping me through this messy divorce. My new friend often spoke how my face was becoming softer and that I now was smiling and even laughing.

I'd tell him about forgiveness and how I prayed for my husband and others who had hurt me. Before we parted ways, he had heard the whole message of Jesus' love for him and His willingness to restore our lives.

He had heard how Jesus with no hesitation accepts those who were lost back into His waiting arms. He heard of grace, mercy, and forgiveness. After many visits, he sheepishly said in a quiet voice, "I think it is time for me to return to a little church that I used to go to. It's time to go back home."

As we said our goodbyes with tear-filled eyes and gentle hugs, we both realized that God obviously had a plan this whole time.

God had provided wood for me but brought a prodigal – a lost but much-loved son – back home.

Jesus lights His fire in us as He fans our smoldering embers of hope, and He often uses mysterious ways and divine encounters to show Himself real to us and others around us.

Always on Time
By Christine Vanderhoff

I woke up for work sounding stuffy. It was only one week into my new job, which was doing exactly what I love: loving on people. I got ready for the day and told myself not to worry. *I never get sick!* However, as the day progressed, my voice slowly disappeared – not OK - since my job requires I talk all day on the phone and on tours. *No, I can't get sick – I'll lose my job!* My concern began to grow into panic. It wasn't long before my boss came in and heard me (or should I say, didn't hear me) and sent me home to check with a doctor.

I'll sleep it off and be fine tomorrow, I assured myself. But when I woke up the next morning, my voice was completely gone.

"This can't be happening. I can't lose this job", I whispered to myself as I picked up the phone to call my boss and then the doctor.

"You have laryngitis and need to rest for two weeks," declared the doctor.

"I can't miss two weeks of work," I pleaded, "I just started this new job and I won't be able to pay my rent!"

"If you continue to talk you may permanently damage your voice," she explained as she wrote a medical excuse for me to take to my boss. She then exited the room, leaving me in panic mode.

Returning to my car I sent a text to my boss with the news, and she quickly responded with encouragement to rest and to get well. Though she eased my concerns about losing my job, paying rent was what loomed heavy over my head and heart.

In tears, I silently cried out to God: *What am I going to do? I can't talk, I can't work, and I have no way to pay my rent!*

I quickly felt God say, "Have I not taken care of you before?" *AWE...OK...so what's the plan?* No answer came.

As long as I can remember, my faith and my finances have walked hand-in-hand. The struggle has always been very real, and I have often questioned God if this was the "testing of my faith." It seemed every time I'd get one step ahead, suddenly I would find myself five steps back – always facing more difficulty. But regardless, I knew that God was real and wasn't going to let me down; my faith and resolve only strengthened in the way He seemed to wait until the "11th hour" most of the time. And here I was again, my faith being stretched to the snapping point.

It was Sunday morning, one week into my doctor-ordered two-week rest, and still no answer had come; rent was due at the end of the week and I didn't have it.

The phone rang, but I ignored it. It rang again. *What crazy person would call me at 7:30 am on a Sunday?* Then someone began banging on my front door. Still half asleep and fuming that someone would dare bug me this early, I pulled myself out of bed to answer the door.

There stood my cousin and his wife, asking if they could come in for a minute. I barely whispered "ok," when he excitedly started to explain that on the way to church they had been talking about me, and felt God direct them to bring me a gift to help toward my rent.

I was stunned as he pulled out three one-hundred dollar bills and handed them to me. I tried to decline this much-needed gift, but he was more persistent than I at this early hour.

He reached over, hugged me and said, "We love you and know that you need this. This is something that God is telling us to do."

They left as quickly as they had come, while I stood just shaking my head in disbelief. I hadn't told anyone that I didn't have rent!

I started to cry as the reality of the answered prayer I'd just received began to set in. As the crisp hundred-dollar bills stared up at me, I reveled over my cousin's faithfulness to hear God's direction.

God's response was like a flood-gate; by the end of the day, two friends had asked me to help them by doing some house cleaning, which would allow me to earn the rest of what I needed to cover my rent. My heart soared and I had a smile on my face that openly declared that MY GOD had once again provided for me when I didn't see a way.

From the scariest and darkest moments to the simplest, He has never let me down. He is always there for me, providing and proving His love. I only need to stop and trust in Him and His plan, for He is always on time.

A Day of Miraculous Multiplication
By J. K. Sanchez

With anticipation, I unlocked the door to the auditorium. Last night a large crew of "little elves" and I had prepared for what looked to be our most successful year for our Holiday Helps program. The food boxes were overflowing, the oversized chest freezer was cram-packed with turkeys, the toy tables were stacked high and we still had a closet full of extras. Plus, in the center of the room stood a 6-foot-tall mountain of donated clothes, in every size possible, waiting for those who would partake in this year's "blessing."

Every family was scheduled so there would be plenty of time for mom, dad or grandparent to shop.

Each able to shop "free of charge" for Christmas gifts and to load up leaf-bags full of clothes for each child in their family. Plus, an added blessing - they would be going home with a holiday box brimming full of food, complete with a turkey.

The love and hours of preparation for this project began way back at the end of August, and today was the day!

The doors opened and the morning began as I had planned, with each appreciative parent that was scheduled appearing as if on cue. But schedules are meant to be broken when it comes to God-appointed appointments, and by mid-morning unscheduled people began to show up, each with broken lives and humble stories. I couldn't say no – I knew HE had sent them and was asking me to believe! Today was a day to stand in faith, not turn any away, and trust in His ability to provide.

The anticipation of something miraculous was stirring and seemed to crackle in the room. The door rattled as the wind blasted it shut and a timid young woman walked in. I was drawn to her hopeless stance and approached her.

She hung her head and looked up at me saying, "I heard you might help me. I have twin 3-year-old girls and I have nothing for them. I don't have an appointment, but if I could just get some clothes?"

I was overwhelmed with her humility and reached out to hug her, "we have plenty, let's shop for them," I encouraged.

For the next hour, with tears spilling from both of us, we found toys and clothes that were just perfect for her twins. But her God-planned perfect miracle was still to come.

We sat on the floor digging through the mountain of clothes. We sorted, and resorted, looking for the correct size.

With great joy the young mom pulled out one beautiful, brand new Christmas dress the exact size for her daughters. But slowly that smile began to change. I watched the smile slowly go out of her eyes as she realized and whispered, "but which one do I give this to?"

"Let's keep looking, maybe there is another pretty dress." I spoke with more faith than I felt, and within my mind I quickly sent up a request for God's hand to provide. As I saw her shake her head in hopelessness I declared, "Let's just take a minute and ask for one."

The shock was obvious – she didn't have a concept of a Father God who would hear her – much less provide for her – but she humbly conceded as I sent up a quick prayer. Off we went in search of more clothes for her girls; by now she was on one side and I on the other of our mountain of clothes. Suddenly, I heard a gasp and a shriek, which catapulted me around the pile to her side.

There she sat dazed – laughing and crying, with the matching dress in the same size, for her other daughter, clutched to her chest. That day changed that mother's life – she saw very clearly that she has a Father God, who does care, hear and provide in twin-size ways.

But the day wasn't over yet, and as the hours passed on, more unexpected families appeared needing our help. I knew the answer was to be YES for each of them; the schedule no longer mattered.

Nearing 3:00 I began to count those who were still scheduled, and realized that we had only packed food boxes for those who had been scheduled. The number of turkeys had also been prepared according to those numbers. My concern now was growing – we would not have enough! Two of my teen helpers were realizing the dilemma as well, and asked me what we were going to do. Again – my response – "Let's ask God to provide."

So, another prayer for provision was lifted, and then I sent them off to count the turkeys, knowing how many we still needed.

Hearing excitement over by the freezer, I approached to find both girls chattering, with eyes as large as saucers, quickly proclaiming how many were left – the exact number of turkeys that were needed for the last group of families coming.

It made no sense – in fact, I had to go look and re-count! But just as they said, they were there on the bottom of the freezer.

Over the next 2 hours, appointments came and unscheduled families *still* filtered in – and now I *knew* we were going to run out; but we gave and gave and gave, and yet the food boxes and turkeys NEVER ran out. As the doors closed and all was finished, one of my volunteers and I lifted the lid of the freezer to find one turkey still there.

With tears streaming down her cheeks, she revealed her need to me. That turkey was there for her and her family, as well.

Oh My God You Are Really REAL

It makes NO sense, but miracles never do! "Whys" will never be answered, but it is enough to know that when we believe – when we say YES and when we love – HE shows up in miraculous ways of multiplication.

(Previously published – *Keeper of the Faith* 2016 Love INC Publishing)

A Roller-Coaster of Divine Provision
By Shellia Reed

The beginning of the new year is usually a time to celebrate and to look to new things that may lay ahead. But for me, it was a time when I suddenly and unexpectedly found myself jobless. Looking back, I never would have anticipated how long I would stay in that state, nor how God would make Himself very real in my life as He provided over and over again in unexpected ways.

My first focus after getting laid off was to apply for unemployment compensation; but to my consternation, I was told that a lag time of approximately six weeks existed between applying for and receiving any funds. As my mind checked off through a six-week span, I knew my reality and that lag time would not match up.

Banks, insurance agencies, credit card, and utility companies all require their timely remunerations.

I was trying to be a woman of faith, but I could feel anxiety begin to ramp up as I viewed my bank account (though there wasn't much to view).

Soon after, at Wednesday evening Bible Study, before the service began, a sweet friend came over to greet me and placed a large manila envelope in my hands. "I've been instructed to deliver this to you," she said. Then she enfolded me in her arms and prayed for me. When I got home and looked in the envelope, I was dumbfounded to find $686.50! To this day I still do not know who gifted that money to me. But due to their obedience to the urging of the Lord, together with the prayers from my friend, I was the recipient of incredible tangible and intangible blessings that night.

I knew that God had called me to go to New Orleans in order to assist hurricane victims. Now that mission trip, which I had planned prior to my layoff, loomed in the forefront of my prayers. I had no income, I didn't see how it was possible – but I stood in faith believing in His provision. No sooner had I begun to ask, He answered.

Quickly my dear friends stepped up and paid for my roundtrip airfare, while others covered my room and board for the entire time I was in New Orleans.

After the first month of God proving and providing faithfully to me over and over again, I had no doubt of His loving ability to provide as my joblessness continued on. He poured out provision in abundance over my life through people who listened and responded – from the old to the young and from those with and those without. He sent groceries, gift cards for gas and food, free haircuts, covered car payments, meals out, movies (with popcorn), and computer use.

Encouragement and love came through prayers, cards and stickers, in large ways and in small ways, and always in astounding ways.

There are so many times when it might seem like God is not working in our lives on a personal level. We have been taught that He always has something better for us, but prayers that seem unanswered can lead to disappointment in even those with the strongest of faith. We wander through life trying to determine what we are doing wrong, hoping to gain God's favor. But the truth is, that we are already in His favor, and He delights to provide for us!

Though His provision may not look like or be presented as we expected, all of it is breathtaking because it all comes from His hand!

As I look back on that jobless nine-month period, I realize that it was a rollercoaster ride that I would not choose to stand in line for again.

However, my connection with the Lord strengthened and grew as I witnessed His loving provision and fulfillment of His promise: "And my God will supply every need of yours according to His riches in glory in Christ Jesus." Philippians 4:19.

True Stories of When God Shows Up

Healing

Matthew 12:15b - He healed them all.

"Jesus didn't pick and choose whom to heal. He healed them all. And he's the same yesterday, today and forever. He heals us all."[1]

Pastor Bob Clark – Crossover Ministries – Parkland, Wa

Oh My God You Are Really REAL

"Call the Doctor – She Can See!"
By Bonnie Simmons

"You will never see again. You most likely won't walk or talk normally, either," the neurologist announced to us.

"Ok. I trust Jesus," I answered.

"You don't understand. You are blind. You won't recover from this. It is permanent," he repeated.

"Ok. I trust Jesus," I said again.

Visibly shaken, he said, "You don't understand! The damage is done. You won't ever see again!"

"Ok. I trust Jesus." I answered yet again. "Are you ok?" I questioned the neurologist, to which he gave no response and stormed out of the room.

Earlier that day I'd suffered a major stroke. Not just any stroke, but one that occurs in only three percent of the population.

It was a bilateral, occipital stroke. 50 percent of all patients die as a result of one, and 99 percent of survivors suffer major physical or mental defects from one.

I was only 50-years-old and extremely healthy; the neurologist ran every conceivable diagnostic test on me but could not find a cause of the stroke. Yet here I lay in the hospital – blind.

I couldn't help but think, "Wow, this is my new normal. What do you want to do in this Lord?" I didn't know if I would live or die. I just trusted Jesus. I kept uttering the words, "No fear. No fear." Later I heard that everyone had thought I was telling myself this – but I let them know I wasn't afraid – I was telling *them* not to fear. God had me – live or die, blind or not. And I really trusted Him with all my heart.

My husband and I never asked God to heal me. We stepped into the place He called us to in that season. We didn't know the outcome; we only knew the Father.

My Pastor and his wife came to the hospital that evening and before they left, he asked if he could pray for me. I told him, "Yes, I trust Jesus."

He prayed a simple prayer of healing, then stood over me and asked, "Can you see me?"

I explained that I saw what looked like a fuzzy, old black-and-white TV outline of him, but no details. Then his wife stood over me and he asked, "Can you see her?" But I couldn't. I also couldn't see when my husband stood over me. Then my pastor stood over me again, and I saw the same fuzzy outline. My pastor said that he was believing God for healing over me, and I responded, "I trust Jesus."

The nurses were in and out of the ICU every hour, testing me and taking care of me. At one point the nurse came in the room and I tracked her with my eyes. She excitedly asked, "Can you see me?" When I replied that I could, she asked, "What time is it?" I answered, "7:00." Shocked, she ran out of the room yelling to the other nurses, "Call the doctor! She can *see!*"

The neurologist came in around 10:00 and asked how I was, to which I replied, "I can see, how are you?" He wasn't very amused and was very matter-of-fact when discussing my recovery. Later that day the nurses had me try to stand up and walk. I stood up, walked and turned in a circle – which actually freaked them out a little. We all laughed about it, thankful that I could walk normally.

The next day the neurologist came in, sat down and shook his head saying, "This could only be a miracle."

I found out from his wife later (she is also a neurologist in the same hospital), that she had been praying for her husband to return to the Lord for some time.

I believe with all my heart that God used this stroke and miraculous recovery to open the eyes of that doctor and return him to the knowledge of Jesus.

I fully recovered within two weeks and, much to everyone's surprise, drove to church just two-and-a-half weeks after the stroke.

Today, several years later, I have no residual complications at all. Whenever I tell someone about the stroke, they really can't believe it happened – but I have the MRI to prove it. I trust Jesus in every part of my life – walking through even the darkest times knowing He's got me.

Riding with the Wind
By Dennis Sanchez

Riding with the wind on my new Honda 300 scooter seemed like a great change from my normal 90-minute drive to work and back – until I found myself lying flat on the floor, experiencing pain so agonizing that I no longer wanted to live.

There was a growing pressure and pain in my neck caused by the consistent wind and the weight of my helmet, but I kept thinking it would begin to subside as my muscles grew accustomed to it. After months of riding with still no resolve, I decided my scooter needed a taller windshield to block more wind, and then my neck would adjust. However, this idea didn't work as I had planned, as the wind now had just a single focus: my head.

One simple drive home from work changed everything – all it took was just a snap in my neck, and the pain was excruciating by the time I reached home.

Day after day, that pain grew even worse. I saw a doctor, but that only resulted in prescriptions for muscle relaxers and pain pills – neither of which helped much anyway. When days turned to weeks, I finally succumbed to my wife's suggestion to see our family chiropractor. I'd get some relief for one or two days following an adjustment, but always be back in nearly intolerable pain again soon after.

As late summer arrived, so did our long-awaited family trip to Glacier National Park. I knew this would require long hours of driving, but I refused to cancel. When the time came, I pushed through the growing pain each day. But each night, as everyone else snuggled into the motor home to sleep, I sat up alone – sipping whiskey, trying to dull the pain enough to sleep.

This is not working, I miserably acknowledged. *This pain is not going away!* Unfortunately, this way of life continued as the leaves began to fall, as the holidays came and went, and all the way through winter.

As I sat in church one Sunday, the pastor began speaking about mountains: mountains in our lives that just wouldn't budge, mountains that block and are overwhelming, as well as mountains that have been placed to stop us from all that God has for us. That's when I knew God had more for me than pain. I soon found myself at the altar – no one praying over me – it was just me and God. I went believing that it was time to cast this mountain into the sea, and that God was my healer. I stood up believing, full of faith, knowing he would heal.

That night the pain was the worst I have ever felt in my life. Even with muscle relaxers, pain pills and whiskey, I found myself wishing I would die to be freed of this pain.

Even in this desperate place, I knew God was my healer and that He had heard me.

As I laid on the living room floor, with pain so unbearable that tears ran down my face, I declared to God, "If this is how I have to live please take me – but I believe you are my healer!"

Sometime during the night while I laid on that floor, my tears of pain changed to tears of praise as I felt the heaviness of His presence enfold me.

His comfort flowed through me. I slowly felt the pain ebb away as I fell into an exhausted sleep.

The next morning as I awoke and lifted my head, I instantly knew something was different: there was NO pain! I jumped up, declaring to my wife, "I am healed! The pain is totally gone!" She looked at my back and excitedly confirmed, "Your back even *looks* different! Where it was curved – it isn't now!" I moved, turned and twisted every way I could, testing if the mountain had really been thrown into the sea.

I continued to "test" over the following week, all while declaring what God had done. Soon after, I saw our chiropractor again and was able to tell him my story. When he looked at my back, excitement bubbled in his voice, "This is not the same spine at all!"

Jesus does heal today, He does hear our prayers and He does cast our mountains into the sea. We just believe and stand in faith through the dark times. That excruciating pain has never returned, and *riding with the wind* is again a thankful joy.

A Birthday Surprise from Jesus
By Dustie Verwers

The sound of crunching metal surrounded me, though it seemed as if it were coming from somewhere else. The pinch in my neck was abrupt, yet disconnected and at a distance. The accident was real – the twisted metal confirmed it was us that had been hit. My stiff muscles, foggy brain and lack of movement were to be expected after an accident – but no one, including myself, knew what was to come from an accident that looked so inconsequential.

Within a few days after the accident, I was seeing my chiropractor daily and began the process of healing – or so I thought. But instead of getting better, I began to experience a growing amount of pain.

Soon I was also seeing massage therapists, physical therapists, an acupuncturist, and had an MRI.

I began feeling confused as to why I wasn't getting better. The nerve pain in my neck continued to intensify.

Months after the accident I was still trying to explain my inability to function to my doctors, and my frustration continued to mount as they turned a deaf ear to my concerns. Hitting a wall, I decided a letter might be a way to get an upfront answer; I documented my symptoms and growing disability and sent it to my chiropractor. However, he responded angrily after receiving it.

"Dustie, you are not disabled. This is all in your head. You are lying." He declared.

I couldn't believe he was saying this and pleaded, "You know me! You know I'm not a liar!" I left that day in tears, not knowing where to turn.

By this time the pain was so intense that I was in need of daily care. I was unable to use my arms to stir a pot of soup, let alone take care of any of my own essential needs. My husband had to shower me and lift me to and from bed. Between my husband and our two teens, much fell on their shoulders – yet compassionately, my family helped me daily.

As a caregiver by nature, I struggled so much to try to do things myself – though I ultimately had no choice but to be humble and receive their care.

Months turned towards years, and I was living on high doses of pain medication – never getting relief nor real answers. The little movement I *could* make, felt like being sealed in a block of concrete or frozen in place.

Finally, in my long pursuit for help, I was directed to a new specialist at Swedish Hospital who diagnosed this living nightmare as "Thoracic Outlet Syndrome."

I was given new hope that my useless hands and arms might function again with the use of Botox injections. Unfortunately, my insurance denied the treatments, and I had no way of paying for the procedure. But, to my sheer disbelief, my doctor jumped in and volunteered to pay for the whole procedure out of his own pocket. A small ray of hope glimmered within me over this amazing gesture! However, my joy was short lived as the Botox wore off after six months, and my arms and hands became useless once more.

Even in the midst of this never-ending struggle, I knew that "My God was faithful, He was good and He was my healer."

Years ago, I had watched Him walk me through a miraculous healing when a bone in my finger was destroyed in an accident. He miraculously restored that bone. I knew He could heal me now – but that healing felt very slow in coming.

Here I sat with discouragement taking a deep hold; between unpaid bills mounting, the marital stress between Donnie and I, and now this newest disappointment – my heart laid heavy in my chest.

My specialist suggested one more option: neck surgery. This surgery would require three muscles to be removed from my neck. Though it was extreme, it was an option – and I desperately took it.

The surgery was performed, but it didn't go as planned. Here I was again – now in even worse shape. I nearly died due to lung impingement. Between nerves, muscles and lungs, my movement had regressed. The pain was so intense I was living on high doses of Morphine, Gabapentin, Oxycodone-Apap, Percocet, Nortriptyline, Tramadol, Flexeril, and Meloxicam just to survive – but with no relief, ever!

For a year I moved as if in a continual nightmare of pain. But finally, ever so slowly, my neck began to respond.

After four years, I was able to take a shower on my own and do other basic things.

But, I was still living on high doses of pain meds, and pain was still a constant companion. I listened continually to the audio Word of God, believing that His hand would somehow be seen through this.

Still hoping for improvement, I visited my doctor. But on this day his words felt more like a life sentence, "Dustie, there is nothing else we can do. We have tried everything that the medical profession knows to do. From this point on, we can try to manage your pain and make you as comfortable as possible." Those words meant living on pain medication in high doses for the rest of my life...just to function.

I knew God was my only answer now. I couldn't live like this.

My birthday was coming up and Donnie asked what I would like.

I looked at Donnie and told him, "All I want is to go to the Todd White Youth Conference." He laughed and said, "You know that we aren't youth, right?"

I knew, but I suddenly felt like the woman in the Bible with the issue of blood needing to just touch Jesus – she knew if she did, then she would be healed. Well, that's how I felt – I knew if I could get there, then I would be healed.

So, my sweet husband said yes and we headed there for my birthday. However, if I had known the reality of the amount of pain I would endure during that conference, I am not sure if my faith would have held out.

As we waited to enter the conference, the rain and cold outside intensified my pain. When we were finally ushered into an overflow room, I was so discouraged I was ready to give up – but something inside me stirred.

The atmosphere indoors was crackling with faith and anticipation of healing.

It was faith that arose inside me, and I knew I needed to get into the main sanctuary. Spontaneously, I got up and moved in, standing at the back – standing through the whole service. As a healing request was announced, I ran forward as far down the aisle as I could get and stood pressed tightly in – shoulder-to-shoulder with hundreds.

As worship began to erupt, I suddenly found myself standing all alone. To me, it was just me and Jesus – the hundreds of us that were physically compacted together didn't matter to me.

I continued to worship – it wasn't about asking for healing or about a man praying for me – it was just about worshiping Jesus.

I was drawn back to reality when I heard from the speaker, "Check your body and see if you have received healing." I moved my neck back and forth, moved my arms and moved my legs – then with exuberance I began to jump up and down.

I literally found myself leaping and jumping and praising God all the way back up the aisle to where my husband stood dumbfounded.

"I am healed!" I shouted. In fact, I couldn't help but declare it over and over – not just that day, but on and on, every day since then - as a declaration that amazes and swells my heart with praise uncontrollable. He is, was and always will be my healer!

I walked out of the conference 100% healed of the spinal nerve injury.

However, I spent six more months walking through the horrible pain of withdrawals. Daily, I chose to walk forward into freedom from drugs.

The high doses of drugs my body was used to surviving on was staggering and required a difficult withdrawal process.

There were days that I was so sick I couldn't lift my head. I experienced intense physical pain that crept over my entire body.

Headaches that were 100 times worse than any migraine I had ever experienced continued to plague me. At times, it felt like it would feel better to rip my skull open to relieve the pain. But within a year, I walked 100% healed: body, soul and spirit, and now in victory over addiction.

During that four and a half years I often thought, "Why did it take so long?" But as I look back now, I am truly thankful for every day I suffered. I honestly would do it all over again. So much growth came to myself and my family through the process.

My children, my husband and I all learned to have compassion and to think about the needs of others in a way that nothing else could have taught us.

It taught us that God truly does meet our every need and that nothing is impossible with God – even when science says it is impossible!

We learned as a family that Romans 8:28 is a scripture we can stand and live on: *And we know that for those who love God all things work together for good, for those who are called according to his purpose.*

Oh My God You Are Really REAL

True Stories of When God Shows Up

Trust

Proverbs 3:5
Trust in the Lord with all your heart, and do not lean on your own understanding.

"Trusting the Lord comes from your heart, not your head. Ignore your head and go to your heart. The Holy Spirit is there enabling you to find a supernatural rest in Christ."[1]

Pastor Bob Clark – Crossover Ministries – Parkland, Wa.

Oh My God You Are Really REAL

Unrelenting Waves of Trust
By Nicholas Smurro

"Trust Me" was all I heard. *I do trust you, Lord! But is that all?* I needed something more, a firm answer – *go on* or *turn back,* or even just *yes* or *no* – I was genuinely and desperately asking because *our lives were at stake!*

We were heading home from a wonderful spring trip – a week of cruising the San Juan Islands for our first time since we'd purchased the boat in the fall. Even though this was the longest and furthest trip we'd taken, it had gone very well – so far – which had contributed to my confidence as the skipper. However, now facing a severe storm, I was calling on God for answers.

We had just cleared the last buoy marking the entrance of the Swinomish Channel into Skagit Bay. Heading south into the wind and waves helped smooth out the ride considerably and allowed us time to gather our thoughts (as well as our legs).

I knew I didn't want to turn back into that narrow channel – the crosswinds and currents were unyielding and we barely made it through without grounding. The next closest port was Oak Harbor, and at a normal cruising speed we could be there in less than an hour. I again asked, "Go on or turn back, Lord?" and immediately heard again, "Trust Me." I decided to continue forward, though my thoughts still pondered, *but is that all?*

My wife handed me my life vest at the same time she threw one to Nolan, our 12-year-old son. I couldn't help but smile inside noticing the wide, carnival-ride-like grin on my son's face as we rose and crested each wave and then dropped forward into the next trough.

I went out on deck and up to the flybridge to make sure everything was tied down. The noise, brutal wind, and stinging cold spray startled my senses.

The severity of this abrupt storm became a brutal reality.

As we rounded Strawberry Point, it was worse than I had anticipated. The wind and waves now crashed on our port side, and I struggled hard at the helm to hold the heading toward the harbor.

The storm was intensifying and periodically a rogue wave tossed us sideways so far that the starboard cabin windows went into and under the water. The boat would immediately roll upright, which was very reassuring, but the contents of cabinets and drawers were strewn about and collecting in the corners of the cabin.

I could see the fear in my wife's eyes as she crouched on the floor of the salon, holding on while holding back tears. Nolan sat consoling her, but I could still see excitement and adventure in his face. His joy gave me strength, and as we locked eyes I thanked him with a smile and nod.

I immediately turned to prayer, "Lord, please calm this storm and get us to port safely. Soon, Lord."

Not a second passed and I again heard, "Trust Me." But just as before, that was all.

Navigational charts showed a buoy marking some shoal hazards just outside the entrance to Oak Harbor. Visibility was poor and radar wouldn't pick it up, so all eyes were searching the rolling seas for the buoy. The waves and winds challenged my ability to hold my bearing straight to the harbor, so we slowly zigzagged toward the entrance.

I attempted to reach the harbor by radio for confirmation of the entrance location, but wind, noise and static prevented that call.

Thankfully, Becky was able to find the marina's phone number, and I dialed it on my cell phone. "Oak Harbor Marina," answered the calm, welcoming voice of Phil, one of the marina employees. I identified our vessel, location and passengers, while Phil quickly helped confirm our position.

With a respite of reassurance, I spotted a red buoy bobbing about 100 yards off. That had to be it. I thanked Phil, hung up and headed toward the buoy. A long sigh of relief and a "finally" feeling came over me.

Unfortunately, relief didn't last long as I suddenly lost all resistance at the wheel. I'd been fighting to keep a heading for hours, so I knew this could only mean the steering was gone. My heart sank as I told Becky and Nolan, and quickly looked for a broken cable or hydraulic leak. Not seeing anything obvious inside the cabin, I headed to the flybridge hoping it still had steering. Finding no response there either, I realized the situation had become extremely dangerous. With the deafening wind, beating rain and relentless rolling, we had no control and were being tossed wherever the sea decided. I prayed, more desperately than before, "Lord, please calm this storm! Fix our steering and get us in!"

Once again, I heard only the words, "Trust Me."

Scrambling down the ladder, I lifted the engine-room hatch to look at the rudder cables and hydraulic lines; all looked okay, so I hurried back inside the salon cabin. I called the marina again to update and inform them we were going to try Vessel Assist for a tow. Upon reaching Vessel Assist and explaining our situation, I was told it would take two hours for them to reach us. That wasn't an option, for we'd drift into the rocks within the hour!

I called the marina again and the Harbormaster, Mack, answered. He had been briefed of our situation and approximate location, and when I told him Vessel Assist's timeline, he reassuringly responded, "We are putting on foul weather gear as we speak, and are on our way."

We were being blown westward toward the bluffs where the charts showed offshore rocks, so we needed to slow our progress toward them while we waited for our rescue.

Using the boat's twin-diesel engines, I tried to twist the bow into the wind by putting one engine in reverse and the other forward. But even with full throttles, the turbulent wind and persistent waves would not allow the bow to come around. I was, however, able to get the stern into the wind, creating a sideways roll that was much easier to handle – except the water coming over the transom was filling the cockpit a lot faster than it was draining. The quickly accumulating water increased weight of the vessel and steadied us a little but was also flooding the boat.

I urgently prayed, "Lord, please don't let us sink!" This time, I immediately heard, "Don't do that!" I knew that meant, "don't put the stern into the waves," (as it was the plain-as-day, obvious thing NOT to do), so I turned the boat again, now having the wind abeam, which stopped water from coming in and allowed the cockpit to drain.

As we waited for rescue, the bluffs grew larger. They now loomed only about 200 yards away – the rocks seeming to beckon us forward. Becky was on the phone with Mack, and he still could not see us.

It was becoming terrifyingly obvious that our rescuers would not reach us before we hit the rocks. I needed to ready the anchor and drop it soon.

I moved forward on deck, low and slow, always holding tightly with at least one hand. A strong wave hit, throwing me against the side of the cabin as the boat rolled about 90 degrees. Regaining my hold, I again pleaded for God to calm this storm. He came back with – you guessed it – "Trust Me."

Scrambling to the foredeck, I attempted to release the clips holding the anchor and chain. The first came easy, but the other was stuck and I was going to need pliers. I made my way back to the cabin, grabbed the pliers, then scurried forward again to the bow.

As I unhooked the clip I thought, *I really don't want to throw anchor in this storm.* But seeing the shore closing in and knowing we would hit rocks first, I started to let out the anchor chain.

As I started to lower the anchor, I suddenly felt a strong sense to look over my right shoulder. Miraculously, a little red blinking light appeared bobbing about 100 yards away. I quickly pulled up the anchor, secured it and drug myself back to the cabin.

Inside, Becky was still on the phone with Mack, just confirming they had spotted us. I grabbed a throw line and made it forward hoping to see the rescue boat on its approach.

What a welcome sight! Mack was standing in the stern of his towboat with a line ready to throw, while Phil brought it to the starboard, downwind side of our much-larger boat. As I held tightly to the bow rail, Mack tossed me his line – but I missed it, as the wind just blew it back to Mack.

Without warning, a huge wave lifted my boat dangerously above the towboat, and I found myself looking straight down on our rescuers. As they settled into a trough, we surfed down the wave straight onto their boat – the thunderous crack easily distinguished despite the howling wind.

As I hung over the rail to inspect the damage, Mack saw the opportunity to throw me a line again. I snagged it with a finger, pulled it onboard and secured it to our bow cleat. I saw Mack yelling into his cell phone – informing Becky that the collision disabled one of the outboard engines on their boat and that they wouldn't be able to give us a tow. I prayed, "Lord, what do we do now?"

Immediately the thought came: *we still have power! We don't necessarily need a tow, we just need steering!*

Mack and I worked together! He pulled our bow in the right direction and kept us on course, as we motored behind and kept the line slightly taut and out of the water and his prop.

After a while we even caught a rhythm with the waves, which kept the boats in sync. Suddenly, as if to highlight our sigh of relief, the intensity of the storm subsided – just as we entered the harbor. Dodging debris and a few drifting docks, we managed to safely make it in and tie up.

What would normally have been a quick jaunt, this unrelenting storm quickly turned into an all-day, desperate ordeal.

During that stormy trial trusting in God had turned the life-threatening outcome into a miraculous one. My God did hear me and did answer my prayers. Admittedly, I was a bit frustrated hearing only, "Trust Me," as it just didn't feel sufficient or definitive enough at the time. But it was. It always is. He knew and He knows.

His protection and provision are always completely sufficient. I realized later that my prayers kept me focused on His help. That focus, kept me at peace as His presence flowed in – which is what truly proved to be my greatest help in the midst of those unrelenting waves.

God's Little House
By Kasey Zeigler

"The worst economy since the depression" was how that economic "slump" had been headlined. If you were trying to buy or sell real estate, you knew it. Houses in my area had been for sale for up to two years with no buyers. My life had taken a left turn into a wall, and I found myself not only on the losing end of a divorce action, but also having to sell my house in this market. However – somehow, someway – God had a plan and a house for me.

I had pretty much accepted my husband's silent treatment that would last for two weeks or more, as well as his belligerent comments (when he did talk). I'd also put up with the way he manipulated situations to put me in a bad light with *his* family, while he consistently kept me away from *my* family and friends.

But this time my husband's anger problem had gotten out of hand: he tried to strangle me in front of our kitchen window, with my neighbor as witness to it all. This I would not allow.

Several days later I sat in a crowded courtroom waiting for my restraining order request to be heard, when a man approached me and asked my name. When I responded, he said, "Thank you, you've been served." And this is how my divorce papers were served to me, with my husband never even showing up. Wow – really? That was beyond awkward.

Once I was home and read the paperwork, I realized that all he was asking for was half of the equity in the home we had shared. He had set himself up financially before he crafted this divorce plan.

Waiting until the last minute to acknowledge his divorce request, I earnestly prayed for an answer. Should I forgive him, humble myself and take him back? Did he even want to come back? Was I being released from my marriage? The only answer I was hearing was, "Don't block his efforts."

With a heavy heart and uncertainty for my future, I signed the papers agreeing to the divorce and liquidation of our home. I trusted God and that He would bring me through this current valley.

Now I had to focus on the selling process of my home, and with wavering concern I began. Nothing was selling! But as I worked with my realtor, he reassured me, "Don't worry. With this market, you will probably still be here in your house 18 months from now." So, the sign was placed and the house went on the market at 7:00pm. By 7:30pm, a showing was booked for the next day. "Wow!" My mind was spinning now, "Well, my God is bigger than the real estate market!"

I left the next morning for an hour while it was being shown. Upon my return all I found was a business card on the counter – but by 4:30pm, my phone rang and my realtor said, "Are you sitting down? You have received a FULL-PRICED offer. FULL asking price, no squabbles or special requests! Now, we need to find you a place to live."

My natural thinking was to pursue an apartment for a while, just to let things settle down and to find my new normal (whatever that was to be). But, God had other plans!

After investigating, it turned out to be less expensive to purchase another small home than to move into an apartment. So, the search began. After touring about 7 houses, there was one that kept jumping out. It was the first one I had looked at – I felt like it was the ONE God wanted me to live in. It was the ONE just for me – it was God's little house.

There it was, I had found it: a cute little 1,100 sq. ft. home that I could call my own, and it was below my price range. The offer was submitted and accepted right away.

Just for me – this was God's little house and I knew it. I always treated it as such, carefully caring for the yard and maintaining, updating and renovating it as needed. Thankful I had been allowed to be its caretaker for as long as HE allowed.

God always provided the money to take care of the necessities, like the roof, new siding and updating the electrical. I was even able to build a new garage!

Then 7 years later, it was time to move on; He asked me to put a sign in front of it.

"What? My little house?" I questioned.

Knowing that He always has the very best for me, I said, "Ok, Lord, I know if you are directing me, then you have a better place for me."

The sign went up and God's little house was sold in just 1 1/2 hours.

My God is bigger and quicker than the real estate market in any economy!

When we trust in His plans, not our own – even amidst the most difficult transitions of our lives – He is always faithful.

Do I Trust God or Man?
By Makalai Michaels

As I looked around my studio apartment, listening to the laughter and joy coming from my guests, I longed for the day laughter would be a regular occurrence in my home. I looked at Rai and thought, *He could be the one. We would have to clean him up a bit but, yes, it is definitely him.* Rai had been my boyfriend for all of two months, but during that time I had fallen head-over-heels for him. I loved him and he loved me, and that was all I needed to know. Laughter continued as the drinks poured and marijuana smoke wafted in from outside.

Looking down, I noticed the stack of unopened mail sitting on my nightstand. It wasn't because I hated bills – as a single woman my cost of living was pretty low – it was more because I just hadn't had the time to open them.

I worked 60 hours a week – and since Rai had come along, nights with him usually ended early in the morning just in time for me to head to work.

As I shuffled through the stack of mail I noticed a letter from my rheumatologist. I had been diagnosed with Lupus four years prior, but I had been off all medications for over a year. However, due to symptoms returning, I'd gone in the week before to have some tests run. As I looked over my results I noticed a test not normally run, labeled "hCG," and in the bottom corner of the paper was written, "YOU'RE PREGNANT." Shocked, I calmly walked over to Rai and handed him the letter he quickly noticed the capital letters.

"Maybe we should step outside," I advised. As soon as we were alone I assertively announced, "I'm not getting an abortion."

He agreed, "Of course not!" And then he pulled me close and whispered in my ear, "I love you."

The next day I saw my gynecologist, Kelly, who'd been my doctor for years and was one of the few who knew about my miscarriage the year before.

I was considered "high risk" because of the miscarriage and Lupus so Kelly immediately put me on light-duty at work with a max of 40 hours. But shortly thereafter, I was fired.

Without employment to take up my time, I began to spend more time with Rai – which included learning how he supported himself. It wasn't long until I was working alongside him, selling drugs and living like a criminally-minded person. Over the next few months I became addicted to the lifestyle and the thrill of victory, I didn't use drugs or alcohol, but this life was my high.

Despite the stress of my criminal lifestyle, I was having a normal pregnancy – until I began showing signs of preterm labor.

I was only six months along. My doctor put me on bed rest for two weeks.

I continued to dilate and was soon presented with orders to be admitted to the antepartum unit at the hospital for preterm labor.

I called Rai, letting him know that I wouldn't be coming home because I had been admitted to the hospital and would be staying until either preterm labor was controlled or until the baby was born.

He sounded concerned over the phone, but a week passed before his first visit materialized, as I waited.

The beginning of my hospital stay was mostly uneventful. I received shots to help develop the baby's lungs and a sonogram every few days. As the days turned into weeks, and even after receiving shots on two separate occasions to stop my labor, my cervix continued to open. After three weeks passed, Kelly decided if I went into labor again, it would be the day I gave birth.

After begging her to let me go home to get some stuff for the baby, she agreed and released me for the night.

Rai picked me up and took me home. I packed a bag for the baby and was able to peacefully fall asleep in my own bed. But that night I had a dream:

> I was lying on the delivery bed. Kelly was sitting between my legs telling me to push, while Rai was on one side and my mother was on the other, both encouraging me to push a little harder. After three long and hard pushes, the baby emerged. It was exactly 9:00 pm and I heard him cry as Kelly announced, "It's a boy! Wow, he is

big! Let's see how much he weighs... 8 pounds, 7 ounces. And 21 inches long." She then asked me if I had a name for him. "J'Bari," I answered, then the dream faded to black.

When I awoke in the morning, I grabbed the calendar and found the current date, February 17. I wrote, *J'Bari, 8 pounds, 7 ounces, 21 inches, 9:00 pm,* as a reminder of the dream, and prepared to return to the hospital.

A week later I was taken for a sonogram; measurements were taken and the technician informed me that my baby's weight was estimated at 13 pounds, and I would need a C-section because the baby would not fit through my birth canal. I informed him of the dream I had, and his response was, "Well, math doesn't lie. You're having a 13-pound baby." Irritated, I politely asked to be returned to my room.

Later a nurse came in with orders to take me to the NICU. "It's more informational than anything," she said to assure me, "All the patients in antepartum go." Once in the NICU I saw babies lying in plastic incubators, some small enough to fit in the palm of my hand.

All the babies were with wires connected to breathing machines and heart monitors. Suddenly, one baby's heart stopped and the nurses had to clear the room. I cried all the way back to my room, as those visions continued to haunt me for days and nights beyond.

Shortly after arriving, my mother came to visit for the first time since I'd been hospitalized. While we sat chatting, I began having very strong contractions.

The nurse came in to check the monitor and I was indeed having labor-inducing contractions. I pleaded with her to make them stop, but she reminded me of my doctor's orders against stopping labor. My mother loudly announced, "You can't do anything to stop the baby. This is going to happen today!" I cried aloud and told her to be quiet.

My mind quickly filled with the not-so-distant memory of the babies on life support in the NICU. I pictured my son with tubes and wires all over his body, stuck in a plastic incubator and unable to be comforted by me. I cried harder.

I pleaded louder, "Please nurse, make it stop! He is not ready. It's not time. This is not what the Lord showed me. Please nurse, please!"

My mother began to yell the opposite, "You're having this baby today, he is coming right now!"

"GET OUT!" I yelled at my mother. Everything and everyone in the room stopped. My mother looked at me confused. My tears stopped and my emotions had hardened. "Get out," I repeated, "I don't want you here – you're not helping."

My mother stiffened and said, "But I am your mother, you can't kick me out."

"Watch me." I turned to the nurse and said, "I want her out of my room. She is causing me undue stress and her presence is not good for the baby." In an angry huff my mother walked out of the room, just as my doctor walked in.

Kelly confirmed that I was in labor, "I don't feel comfortable giving you something to stop the contractions, as we have already done that twice in the past month. If this baby wants out today, then he is coming out today."

I began to cry, "This is not what the Lord showed me!"

"What do you mean?" She asked.

"Well," I began, "the night you let me go home I was given a dream by the Lord of my entire birthing process.

The Lord gave me a name and told me exactly what time he would be born, as well as his weight and length. None of this is what he showed me." I continued to sob.

Kelly grabbed my hand and gently looking into my eyes she said, "Believe who you want. You can trust me – your doctor – or you can trust the God of the universe. Believe who you want."

She released my hand and turned to my nurse saying, "I'll be back to check on her in an hour. Page me if anything changes." Then she and the nurse left.

As I sat alone in my room I replayed the words of my doctor, *"believe who you want"*. I closed my eyes and prayed to the Lord. I told Him I not only remembered the dream, but I was choosing to believe the dream. I was choosing to believe His version of the story. I didn't end with amen – instead I drifted off to a peaceful sleep. Sometime later my nurse came into check me; my contractions had stopped and both I and the baby were sleeping.

When my doctor returned she confirmed my contractions had stopped. "Well," Kelly said to me, "Maybe it's not today after all." I gave a groggy nod and went back to sleep.

As I remained in the hospital, my 48-hour sonograms continued and I was no longer bothered by the comments of the technicians.

I chose to believe the Lord. I was just happy to be able to see my baby developing. After 10 days of no contractions nor signs of labor, I was allowed to go home.

Once home, the weeks passed on and I quickly forgot the dream the Lord had given me. It now seemed I was going to be overdue. We tried all the tricks to get things moving again, but he would not budge. The Monday before his due date, Kelly informed me she would be on-call Friday and if I had not delivered yet, we would induce. I went home and began to prepare myself for his imminent arrival. Monday through Thursday my body saw no action.

On Friday, overdue by TWO days, I arrived at the hospital.

A friend arrived with me and stayed while I got situated and began the induction; however, she left about two hours later and for the next five hours I labored alone – no "loving boyfriend" in sight.

Luckily, I had a nice delivery nurse to keep me company, comfortable and calm. Around 6:30 pm, family members began to show up, and yes – even my mother was allowed in the room.

Right as I became fully dilated, my "loving boyfriend" finally arrived. With mother on my left and boyfriend on my right, I pushed my son into the world. Kelly was the first person to lay eyes on his physical form, and as I heard my son's first cry I suddenly remembered the dream the Lord gave me. "What time is it?" I shouted. "9 p.m." the nurse responded. "How much does he weigh?" I yelled back.

"He is 8 pounds, 7 ounces. And 21 inches long." "Thank you Jesus!" I yelled.

I instantly realized the dream had come to pass exactly how the Lord had shown me. The impact of this event has shaped my trust in the Lord.

Though I had turned my back on the Lord and insisted on going my own way, He did not turn His back on me. He gave me a dream to sustain me as I faced one of the most difficult times in my life.

I also learned when God gives us a dream or vision of our life, it is tested by those around us. I had two choices at that time: to trust God or Man. I could make a choice to believe my doctors and family members who were experienced in the field and wanted the best for me, OR to trust and believe God. Without this dream to hold on to, I would have spent energy on something beyond my control. However, once I chose to believe God, I had a peace beyond all understanding.

True Stories of When God Shows Up

Protection

Psalm 91:4
Under his wings you will find refuge.

"There is no defender like our God. No protector like our Savior. He is built to shelter you. He has wings to provide you shelter."[1]

Pastor Bob Clark – Crossover Ministries – Parkland, Wa

Oh My God You Are Really REAL

His Reinforced Shelter
By Kasey Zeigler

For nearly a year I had been living in the village right outside the base gates. My house was one of mortar-less cinder blocks, built up around a beautiful marble floor. There were no modern buildings or everyday conveniences here. Oh, how I craved hot water without having to build a fire. Today, just like many others, I watched the new farm tractor pull the wagon filled with men, heading to the fields – ready for a day of hand-tilling the land; my thoughts repeated the well-known phrase "two-thousand years of civilization unmarred by progress." This was Turkey with its nearly 100-degree year-round temperatures and overly bright sunshine.

Here I have been walking in the middle of the region where St. Paul had preached to the Gentiles.

My reignited walk with Jesus was stirred as I saw this country's beauty; from Mersin beach on the Mediterranean Sea to St. Peter's Grotto in Antalya. My enjoyment was expanded as I found myself spending much time in Tarsus (St. Paul's birthplace) and Ephesus. But my time here was coming to an end.

I was informed that my security clearance would need to be re-established for the job I would be soon transitioning to in my next assignment; I would need to travel to Germany for five days to accomplish this.

Germany had been very unsettled against the military presence since the deployment of mid-range missiles in the early 1980's, and there had been many thwarted terrorist attacks, and even one successful one just 5 years ago. However, I was not fearful to travel to Germany, even alone. So off I went, anticipating accomplishment of what was needed for my upcoming move – never expecting what would unravel within a few short days of my arrival.

Upon arrival, my testing was completed much quicker than expected, which left me with several free days. Since my brother was stationed nearby, I excitedly anticipated a visit and headed to the train station for a ticket to Frankfurt.

I quickly sent word to Christopher of my arrival plans. Upon arriving in Frankfurt, I took a few minutes to get my bearings, as this was my first visit to this town. Reaching for my checkbook in preparation of acquiring a taxi across the base, I realized it was missing! I thought I had been smart! I knew I could be an easy target for pick pockets, so I had hidden my funds in the sleeve of my checkbook and slid it into the inside pocket of my jacket. But I had still been robbed. Somehow in the hustle and bustle of people on the platform at the Wiesbaden station, my $400 for my once-in-a-lifetime visit was now gone! I found the Red Cross office and told them my story, but quickly discovered that I didn't fit their criteria for help.

In exasperation I questioned, "Oh, Lord, what do I do now?"

Here I was in Germany, without a penny to my name, at a time when cell phones and ATM cards weren't around. The young man at the Red Cross counter sensed my true need, and opened his own wallet and gave me $20.00. Humbled, I took his address to repay him once I returned to Turkey.

He let me use the phone in his office to call my brother, and soon after Christopher came walking in with his co-worker, both in military police uniforms. Trying to be inconspicuous, I walked out with these two tall MPs and got into the back of their police car for the ride over to Rhein-Main AFB! I can only imagine what those around the area thought as they watched us leave.

I was soon relieved to be settled into a room and treated to dinner by my brother. It was too late to reach my American bank, so everything would have to wait till tomorrow.

"Okay, Lord, I know you have me. What else could possibly happen?" I whispered as I settled in for sleep.

Considering the events of the day, I slept surprisingly well and woke to the sound of the girl in the adjoining room using the lavatory. "How long is she going to take?" I thought as I laid there. Finally, I heard her go back to her room and exit into the hallway. Glancing at the clock on the table: 7:14 am. I ran to the bathroom. I no sooner sat down when I heard a tremendous explosion and black smoke surrounded me.

After what seemed like an eternity, I began to hear muffled cries and shouts from both inside and outside of the building. I stood slowly and took an assessment. I found nothing missing or even injured on my personal being.

"Thank you Jesus!" I exclaimed as I quickly dressed in the clothes I had brought in with me. As my senses slowly returned, I became aware of frantic cries of my name being shouted by several voices.

My thoughts raced, "My brother! What has happened?" I opened the door from the bathroom into the room I had slept in last night – there were no walls between the parking lot and me.

Glass was strewn all over the bed I had just exited moments before. I made my way through the wreckage to the hallway just as Christopher and two others were approaching, shouting my name. Christopher grabbed my hand and got me out of the building. As the smoke subsided the grisly aftermath was revealed: where cars had previously been, the parking lot was now covered in burned, twisted metal.

I later learned that two people had lost their lives and that the '76 green Volkswagen parked near my windows was used as a car bomb.

The whole side of the building was gone, except the lavatories that were somehow reinforced. But I was alive!

Had I lounged in that bed for half a minute more, I couldn't say that I would be here now.

God knew the exact time and place to move me to safety – an unexpected shelter that would save my life.

A Phantom Train
By Stacy Wind

Our road home was blocked as the railroad crossing arms slowly began their descent, with red flashing lights signaling an approaching train. But instead of an unexpected interruption simply slowing our progression home, the situation quickly turned strange – like a scene from a Twilight Zone episode!

It was late – 1:00 am to be exact – with only a few miles from home and our warm bed. We sat waiting and waiting, but no train passed. The crossing arms still down, lights flashing, and the obnoxious "ding ding ding" piercing through the eerily quiet night air. But as we continued to wait, still no train came. Then, just as suddenly as it began, it was over.

The lights quit flashing, the sound ceased and the crossing arms lifted – no train had ever crossed or been seen. Strange!

Then "strange" turned into "reality" just one block ahead. An accident had just occurred at the intersection – a pickup truck crashed head-on into a light pole. The reality of our "Twilight Zone episode" presented very clearly; we both realized that our phantom, non-existent train had provided us safety.

If we had not been stopped at that railroad crossing, we would have been in that intersection at the exact moment the pickup truck came careening through.

God's specific hand of protection reached down, dropped those railroad-crossing arms in front of us, and stopped what may have taken our lives. I know that the love of my God saved our lives that night in a strange, but very real way.

<u>Intermission</u>

Movies, concerts, and theater productions have historically offered a time of intermission between segments of their entertainment. This intermission gives us a time to process; to take an emotional break and to share or compare with others about our experience. Today, I stretch the intermission philosophy to include this little book.

Take a short intermission here and consider your life. Process these previous stories through your current paradigm of who God is, who Jesus Christ is, and who the Holy Spirit is. Think through times in your life where you have also experienced what you may have quickly swept away as "coincidental" – is it possible that these times could have instead been when a very REAL God was stepping in and "showing up" on your behalf?

As you have read the previous stories, have you found yourself saying, "Oh My God"? These stories are all true and may seem to be beyond your comprehension of the God you personally understand. If so, you are in exactly the right place.

During this little break between stories I want to share with you a gift – one free of charge and specifically available to you right where you sit.

This same God you are reading about sent His son to make a way for you to enter heaven – and He is the gift. No strings attached – He offers this gift to you right now. You need only to believe, ask, and receive the gift. The gift of forgiveness is yours – reach out and receive it. Total forgiveness – unearned and undeserved – will be handed to you upon acceptance.

John 3:16 "For God so loved the world, that He gave His only Son, that whoever believes in Him should not perish but have eternal life."

It really is that simple! His love for you was poured out before you were ever born. He knew all your sins before they were committed, yet He has already forgiven them. He waits ready to receive you, to give you a freedom that is inexplicable and full of joy.

Do you desire a relationship with a real, loving and good God? If so, simply believe and ask – your life will never be the same. His presence will flood in and begin a transformation that will forever open your eyes to say, "Oh My God, You are really REAL."

True Stories of When God Shows Up

Forgiveness

Colossians 3:13
Forgiving each other; as the Lord
has forgiven you.

"Forgiveness comes out of being forgiven. The more aware you are of God's unfailing, unending love for you... the more ability you have to pass it on!" [1]

Pastor Bob Clark – Crossover Ministries – Parkland, Wa.

Oh My God You Are Really REAL

Out of the Ashes – Forgiveness Rises
By Donna Jackson

A blazing torch was shooting 60 feet into the air, while black smoke curled even higher. Signaling for miles, a part of my life was unmercifully being consumed.

I had been given a nice, quiet evening of dinner preparation, while Mike took the kids to softball practice. But the quiet was shattered when the dogs erupted with barking as someone began banging on my door, shouting, "Fire! Get out of the house! I've called 911!" Without thinking, I herded my dogs out the door and scooped them into the car. Turning to see a pillar of fire like I have never seen before – coming from the corner of my back yard.

My family and the fire truck arrived almost at the same time. Containment was swift, as the only thing destroyed was one tree in the corner of the yard.

But the loss of that tree was as if my heart had been smashed – it held memories of life and family for over 22 years. It was the first tiny tree planted in our first home and had grown to be a beautiful and stately 60-foot pine tree, as our son and daughter also grew. At only five-and seven-years-old, my children had worked with my husband to build a beautiful tree house in that tree – they had a wonderful time helping Daddy build it every day for weeks. Our whole family enjoyed that tree house – the wooden ladder got us up high enough to see all over the city, and the wonderful slide was fun to ride down. Life happened in that tree house! Now it was smoke, ash and a charred, burned-out stump – and it left a gaping hole in my heart.

With no found cause for the fire, our search for understanding kept this destructive emptiness open like a wound that would not heal. We knew in our souls that the mentally-unstable elderly woman next door had something to do with it.

She had requested we cut down our pine tree because it dropped pine needles in her yard that she believed caused her cancer.

Even after we cut all parts of the tree that were anywhere near her side of the fence in an attempt to accommodate her unseemly request, her words had taken root in my heart and suspicious mind – even more so as I looked out at the charred, burned-out stump that held so many memories.

My broken heart could not believe any other reason for the tree catching fire. My heart was unforgiving, and days turned into weeks of anger simmering over this loss. "How did I get to this place?" I cried out to God, as I realized that my thoughts were now consumed by hate. I finally asked God, "How do I get out from under this?"

As these questions turned to prayer, I felt the Lord nudge me to go out to that charred, burned-out tree stump – to lay my hand on it and pray FOR my neighbor!

"Really, God? Pray for her? Right now, I don't feel like I could speak her name, much less pray for her." Hate is a harsh word, but right then that was what I felt for her.

After my (not so nice) discussion with God, I complied with what He told me.

My ugly, black heart raised its head even while praying, but I continued to tell God my feelings and my pain.

Every day I continued this process of praying for my neighbor, Linda. I prayed for God to forgive me for feeling this anger and to forgive her if she had been responsible for this. I prayed and cried beside my burned-out tree stump for many days, many weeks.

I cried for the loss of years of love for that first little tree. I cried for the memory of how hard my husband and children worked to build the tree house. I cried for the way I felt that someone could be so mean that they could do something so hateful.

Every day I prayed a little differently, and every day my heart became a little lighter. It became easier to pray for my neighbor. I felt the anger and hatred slowly disappear and change into compassion toward her. A month passed, and I realized I felt relief and could let it go completely – I was able to forgive. Two months passed, and one day she came to my door with a basket of peaches from her peach tree, and I was able to accept them with joy!

I had made peace and had forgiven her, and now realized why God had asked me to pray each day for my neighbor.

Several more months passed, and my weeping time at the stump had changed my heart.

One day I noticed a little tree growing near my burned-out tree stump, and as I turned I found two more trees growing along the fence. I decided to water them, curious to see how they'd grow. As they began to get big leaves, I searched information on trees and discovered my new little seedlings were fig trees – three perfect little fig trees.

In place of my one pine tree, God had blessed me with new life – not one but three trees, and trees that would one day be full of abundant fruit.

Those fig trees grew rapidly, and I was blessed by an abundance of fresh figs – and was even able to share them with my neighbor before she passed. Fig trees planted for me by the hand of God: they were a gift, a smile from my Heavenly Father, a blessing because of obedience found in a choice to forgive! Those fig trees where nourished and strengthened by the burned-out pine tree's sacrifice.

Now, many years later, I still have those fig trees that bless me every year with an abundance of fruit.

I look at my three huge fig trees today as they shade my backyard beautifully; they bless all the birds with shelter and food and bless us with their fruit.

I am reminded that my God is good and faithful all the time. He pours out His blessings when I listen and follow His lead in my life. He knows best for me even in the midst of darkness and pain!

He will always bring blessing and joy out of the ash if I look to Him. Forgiveness will always bring me back to a place that He desires for me, a place of freedom - a place of peace and plenty.

A Road to Murder
By Randy Love

With a .38 revolver on the passenger side of my truck, 98 miles was all that stood between me and the man I was set to kill. In 90 minutes my life would change forever.

Decades ago, I moved from Springfield back to the Central Oregon Coast where I was raised. My mother needed help financially, and my move was the answer. Upon returning home, I started up a general maintenance business, and Mom worked with me painting houses. We made a great team.

Not long after arriving, I'd found out that Mom had been writing to a man in prison through a pen pal program (I'll call him 'Bob').

Mom is a very kind-hearted person who would help anyone, and at Bob's release from prison she immediately invited him to stay with us while he got on his feet.

Long story short, Bob swept her off her feet and they were married. He joined us in the business, and we worked together well. Like me, he could fix anything. We began taking on bigger jobs and making more money, and he proved to be a real asset. I had easily set up credit accounts at the local hardware and lumber stores, as everyone knew me and my integrity; as my trust in Bob grew, I began adding his name to the accounts so he could also pick up supplies or tools as needed.

Just as everything seemed like it was going great, life took a dive for Bob. He started drinking – HEAVILY. Empty whiskey bottles were showing up in the garage, bathroom, kitchen cabinets, truck, and anywhere you looked – including the job sites. He was unraveling quickly and it showed up in every job he worked on. It was destroying the business relationships that had been built over the years and my reputation as an "honorable and trustworthy local boy" was quickly swirling the bowl. In the process, the destruction hit our personal lives.

One day the "sheetrock hit the fan."

In a drunken rage, Bob had torn out the living room wall of our five-year-old home and left it in pieces with scattered debris everywhere. I found Bob passed out in the bedroom, and I woke him out of his stupor. Profanities flew from him as I yelled at him, trying to understand why he would do such a thing. He screamed back, "I thought you wanted a bigger front room! So, I did it!" With 2x4s and sheetrock thrown across the living room and adjacent bedroom, it looked like a battle zone!

Arriving home to the mess, Mom burst into tears. The hurt and disbelief on her face broke my heart.

My nerves were shot, and my patience was dwindling; and now my heart hurt. Not only was the mess of our home and business heavy on my heart, but seeing how badly he treated Mom was overwhelming. Once elegant and proud, this woman was now emotionally beaten. I watched her do a lot of praying through this storm, hoping the nightmare would stop, but it seemed like the Heavens were closed.

The next storm had already brewed, and was ready to hit with a vengeance. Bob took off with my work truck, saying he had a job nearby.

Mom and I were relieved that we had some time to process this insanity. But one day turned into two, and then three.

Where is my truck? I've got work to do. My frustration turned into disbelief when I received a phone call from the lumber and hardware stores informing me that my accounts were maxed out. To my horror, I found that Bob had purchased tools and supplies, then resold them dirt-cheap so he could keep his booze binge going.

I was enraged. ENRAGED!!! I drove the 15 miles to Bob's parents' house to try to track him down. They too were drinkers and dishonorable folks, and as I banged hard on their front door, his dad, half-drunk, opened it just as I saw Bob run out the back door. *You coward!* I thought to myself. My adrenalin shot through my veins as I pushed the front door aside to chase Bob. His dad pulled a .357 handgun from under a pillow and pointed it right at me.

I stared at him with rage and could see the fear in his eyes. What do you do when the person at the end of the gun barrel isn't afraid? I wasn't, and it terrified him. I did not budge an inch as he yelled at me.

I continued to stare him down as he stepped forward and stuck the barrel of the gun in my gut. The tension was thick as his demands only solidified my determination to get what I came for: his son and my work truck.

"You're a coward just like your son. You don't have the guts to pull the trigger!" I yelled in his face.

As I turned my back on him to head back out the front door, I heard my work truck drive away. I glanced back at the old man as he lowered his gun.

As I drove home, adrenaline was pulsing through my veins and my heart was beating so fast I thought it might explode. Still furious, I was trying to calm down and struggling to process all that had just happened.

Unbeknownst to me, Bob had one last storm brewing.

As I pulled into my driveway, I saw my work truck was back. *What is Bob doing here?* I wondered, pulling in closely behind the truck to ensure he would not take it again.

I was shocked and dismayed as I realized Mom's car was gone. This was not just any car!

I'd spent six months restoring this "baby," and gave it to Mom for Christmas when I was finished. I was very proud of it and Mom loved it!

How could I recover from the multiple disasters that had just blown through our lives?

In just 8 short months our lives were in shambles. Our house was destroyed, our home-life was a mess, and our business was struggling – Bob stealing Mom's prized car was the straw that broke the camel's back.

Over the next month I began the process of partial recovery: I fixed up the house to sell, closed the business, and set up payment plans to repay the local businesses where Bob had racked up debt in my name. Mom moved to Washington to take care of her stepdad and I moved to Portland and took a job with a security company.

I worked nights, which gave me a lot of time to think – a lot! My sweet, fun-loving and kind nature was gone. It was replaced by anger, resentment, shame, hate, and bitterness, all topped with a bit of self-pity. I lived in this miry mess of emotions for months, allowing it to simmer. I was on a downward spiral as I focused on Bob and the aftermath of his destruction.

GONE...everything we had worked so hard for was ruined and gone. My mind constantly replayed the chain of events. I knew that Bob needed to pay for destroying our lives.

I'd made up my mind: I was going to kill him and nothing was going to stop me. Today was the day I would make him pay!

I got off work at 6:00 am, drove to my apartment, changed clothes, and placed my gun on the front seat of my truck. As I started my drive from Portland to the Coast, 98 miles was all that stood between me and the man I was going to kill.

I was determined to find Bob and make him sorry he had ever met us. Mile after mile I looked at the gun, and visualized shooting him – not even caring about consequences.

Arriving at the Coast, I was a mess; my blood pressure was peaking, my heart was racing, and my soul was filled with hatred. But I just wanted it done and finished, as though it would bring me closure.

When I was just five minutes away from Bob's parents' house, my truck cab suddenly began filling with a fog. I instantly knew this was a spiritual event, and that God was stepping in.

He opened my eyes to what I had allowed my soul to become. I was a Christian, yet consumed by a murderous spirit.

Literally minutes away from killing a man, I began crying out to God to forgive me for what I had allowed myself to become. I cried out, "Lord, how do I turn this around?"

Coming to a place where I could turn my truck around and head away from my original destination, the tears flowed and I began to feel the bitterness seeping out of my heart.

Again, and again I sobbed, "How do I turn this around?" Then deep inside my heart I heard, "Every time you think of Bob, pray for him."

I prayed for Bob every way I could think of – for his wellbeing, for his heart to be set free, for his dad and mom, and for deliverance from alcoholism. I continued to pray in the months to come, asking God's help when my mind would stir up past hurts, and I would again begin to pray for Bob.

Bob never knew how close he came to his life being taken that day or how the depths of bitterness and a road to murder had begun rotting my soul.

I am grateful for my life-changing encounter with God. I learned a lot through that process.

I learned that choosing to forgive and praying for your enemies keeps your heart tender and saves lives (others, and, your own).

I learned what *love your enemies* means, as God changed my hate for Bob into genuine love.

I learned that God knows our hearts, does step in to make Himself real, and can turn around the impossible.

A Choice to Forgive
By C. Marie

Trust is a word that only becomes real when it has been shattered and tested in your life. At the age of 16, trust of a "grandfatherly" man should mean being left alone with them is safe; however, this is not always the case.

On the infamous day where trust was shattered in my life, it was snowing and cold and my grandmother and sister coaxed me to go along as they delivered Christmas cards to the elderly. Walking in the cold was not on my agenda that day; I wanted to stay warm inside, so I stayed at the house with "that man."

It seemed a little odd when he sat next to me on the couch, but warning lights didn't begin to flash just yet. But when I tried to get up from the couch and he pulled me back down, those warning lights began blaring. He proceeded to hold and caress me in all the places that were NOT OK for him to touch.

"STOP!" I yelled several times, not understanding how this could be happening.

"If you tell anyone, I will deny it," he whispered in my ear as he continued.

As my grandmother and sister returned, he jumped up and moved back to his chair. The dramatic movement caused a slight confused look to pass between me and my grandmother. I jumped up, grabbed my coat and headed out the door as I said, "I'm walking home."

Walking the mile home gave me time to cry and question God. I didn't understand why this had just happened or what to do. I knew it was wrong, and by the time I reached home I knew I couldn't keep quiet.

"Dad, I need to talk to you," I said. Explaining the situation and the outcome was extremely hard. Harder yet was his response, "What did you do to make him do that to you?"

My mind was spinning, the tears began to run. *What? I don't understand this! I am being blamed for this?* My heart was fracturing into pieces, as he walked away and headed out to pick up Mom.

I had begun the day an innocent and trusting teen, but by the end of the day all of that had been crushed. My Dad, Mom and grandmother all sided with the lies "that man" told, even expecting me to apologize for what I had said about him. My life took a turn that day, and for the next 16 years my heart became the harbor of insecurity and unforgiveness. Trust was banished to the depths of that lonely harbor.

During those years my faith and love for Christ grew; He was my safe harbor – the only one I could depend on, the only one I decided I could trust. Then a day came when God spoke to me deep inside my heart and asked me to do something I didn't think I could do: forgive that man. I surely didn't want to!

Several weeks later a conversation with my Mom turned in an unexpected way, as she told me "that man" had terminal cancer. As she went on to explain, my own thoughts seemed to muffle out the details. *I really don't care. I don't wish cancer on anyone, but it sure feels like he deserves it for what he did to me.* I hung up those thoughts as I hung up the phone.

However, God didn't hang up. I heard God speak to my heart, "Don't let him win."

Oh, man – I knew I was in trouble.

I spent two weeks fighting that voice, finally giving into the strong urge from Jesus to pick up the phone and call him. *Ugh.*

As the phone in the hospital room rang, I swallowed hard.

He answered in a rough, gravelly voice, and I quickly explained who I was and before he could respond. I said, "Don't talk, I need to do this." With those few words spoken, a peace enveloped me, my heart slowed and my words became concise – not my words, but His words.

"I need to tell you that I forgive you. I have been harboring feelings of hurt and anger for so long, and they have robbed me. But these feelings end today. I forgive you and I want you to die in peace knowing that I no longer hold this over your head or in my heart. I know that you know what you did was wrong, and it is time to let it go. I forgive you and love you." I stopped talking and heard nothing until faint sounds of crying became audible. He finally acknowledged his wrong-doing and said he was sorry. Our call ended as I again expressed that I forgave him and loved him.

I am thankful that I listened to Jesus' urging and chose to forgive him, for within two short weeks he passed away – but he was able to pass with a peace that previously had been devoid.

Finding forgiveness started with the soft whisper from Jesus to my heart.

Completion of the process required a choice – the hardest choice I have ever made.

This choice brought another into a place of freedom from guilt, but also brought me a new-found freedom, victory, peace and joy that had been stolen 16 years before.

I now know that trust is found as we find what forgiveness really is; as we walk through the tests of life and bring those to the cross of Jesus. He is one I can trust every day and, in every way, because He never changes. Jesus is the same yesterday, today and forever.

Love

1 Corinthians 13:13 - The greatest of these is love.

"Our love for God is weak. But his love for us is greater than all! It's by the love of Christ that we love. The greatest thing we can do is receive God's great love for us!"[1]

Pastor Bob Clark – Crossover Ministries – Parkland, Wa

Oh My God You Are Really REAL

Two Love-hungry Hearts
By Melissa Lee

As the landing gear hit the tarmac, I was jolted back to reality as the pilot announced, "Ladies and Gentlemen, this is your Captain. On behalf of your crew and Alaska Airlines, I want to thank you for flying with us. We hope you have a wonderful stay in Seattle, Washington, and that you choose us again for your next travel destination."

Welcome to Seattle? WELCOME? Just one month ago I boarded a flight with a one-way ticket to "No More Sorrowsville" a.k.a. El Paso Texas. I had determined the past was behind me and come what may – I would move forward from the grief gripping my soul. I would board my flight, land in Texas, and would move on. I would leave her graveside, and somehow begin again.

Little did I know that pain and grief had joined me on board and stowed away in my heart, along with a familiar, yet distant companion, God.

I had only been gone a month, with only a year since I had stood at my Mother's graveside.

Now, as my thoughts plummeted at the same speed as my heart, every step into the terminal brought me closer to my father and my reason for return. My father had summoned me home – with the announcement of cancer's impending battle for his life. What I would discover in the next year would forever shift the landscape of my heart.

As I threaded through the arrival obstacles, my thoughts drifted unchecked. My familiar friends, pain and grief, raised their heads and whispered in my ear, "Why did I even come home?" My groping mind and heart questioned, "Was God still here with me? Or did He miss the flight? Was I really going to have to face this one on my own? Could I face my father alone, the one who hurt my heart so deeply?"

Even with all this chaos swirling in my heart, something awakened within me that day.

I can never fully explain what took place, but it is here that I offer my best explanation. God was about to do a work in each of us that would restore His original design.

He awakened love and a miraculous transformation would begin over the first 90 days and come to fruition within exactly one year.

My father had been seeing a counselor when I arrived home, and the obvious fruit became an inspiration to me (though I wouldn't tell him that yet). Observing what seemed his success with the counselor, my thoughts began reminiscing about my father, my childhood, and current emotional predicament. They settled on one phrase that had been played over and over growing up: "you remind me of your dad." I knew that wasn't a positive remark since yelling, spanking, and distancing himself emotionally from me was the way I assumed he had determined to get *him* out of me.

Even Dad had said that I reminded him of himself and he wanted better for me, but I could never figure out how to get that. All I remember was that I was in trouble, never measured up, and he *didn't want me, didn't like me,* and certainly *didn't love me*; this was my "mature" 8-year-old thinking. But, like any other daughter, I did want my father's approval and worked hard to be different to gain it.

This desire for approval unfortunately followed suit in my newly found relationship with Jesus and God, but was of no effect on my father. At this point, I dismissed my dad from my heart, and moved on with life (or so I thought).

As a lover of Jesus and an alcoholic, my father used this substance to quiet the rage inside; his pain and grief being muted, but not healed. He was present physically, but distant emotionally; yet his love for Jesus was deep-seated. Soon after my mother's death, he realized he was all his daughters had left and checked into an in-patient treatment center.

He invited my sisters and me to be part of his healing process, which began turning into *our* healing process, as well. Something shifted when he arrived home from treatment; he was more sensitive and his heart was available to me in a way that was both scary and exhilarating. I began to consider, "Could it be that he really did love me?" His heart also began to open more fully to God, as he was honest with himself and me about what had transpired over many years.

Remembering the past stirred a desire for transformative fruit in my life, as well, and I found myself in the counseling office.

Something unique began to unfold as I began the process, too. My dad and I found ourselves on a similar appointment schedule, and evenings started to become lengthy discussions of what had surfaced. God began reconciling our hearts and revealing the love we had for one another that had been veiled by our pain.

I began to hear "I love you Missy," and then one night, everything changed. As I sat speaking with him about my day, he became silent with tears streaming down his face. He saw me with his heart that night, embraced me and asked for forgiveness. Forgiveness for the years of hurt and pain he had caused, and then he simply asked, "Missy, can I take you out for dinner and bowling?" I sat *dumbfounded* as my love tank began to be filled to overflowing after so many years running on empty. God was on the move in our hearts! In 90 short days together, God had done it! He had brought restoration to two wounded hearts.

We went bowling, and then to dinner several nights later. There were many more beautiful moments together over the next nine months.

When I sat next to my dad, holding his hand and saying goodbye as the cancer had taken over, I knew that this girl's heart was full of love from and for her father. I knew my dad would finally have his heart filled with an eternal love, wiping away every tear he had ever cried.

What God had planned before the beginning of time found a place to manifest in two hearts hungry for love. It was these 12 months of life that awakened my heart not only to my earthly father, but most importantly, my Heavenly Father. Exactly one year to the day of stepping off that plane in Seattle, I said goodbye to my earthly father. God had reconciled and healed our hearts, and now with confidence I believe that He can do the same for others.

God's desire is to reconcile hearts back to himself. May the God of reconciliation fill you with Hope, may the God of reconciliation strengthen and encourage your heart in your moments of deepest sorrow, and may you open your heart to the God of reconciliation who has a plan and purpose for your life that is beyond understanding. Now is the time – for you are loved!

Love Found in the Desert
By Lorena Hartzog

The desert? Who moves there? My churning thoughts continued to struggle with our upcoming move. Our business of 30 years had recently closed and the exhausting, labor-intensive packing had been going on for weeks, and now we were almost ready to load up and drive away.

My husband had grown up in the desert – in fact, the same area we were now moving to. His dream of moving home was coming true; however, this was not my dream.

We had spent 30 years building a flourishing nursery business, caring and tending to glorious plant life on the "green" side of Washington. I loved the green and the rain that made it that way. We had made a life here – great friends, family and church – I fit in here and it was MY home.

Giving that all up and moving to the "brown" side of Washington – a desolate, dry desert – was such a struggle. But I trusted God and I knew He would show Himself strong in my life. Like it or not, the move was on so off we went. *I am headed for the wilderness.*

Settling in was a lonely process for me. I love to talk and laugh. I just love people and this new desert place was different! I felt isolated and had many prayerful conversations with God. I asked many times for His provision of friends and a way to show the love of Jesus to others in my new desert home.

About three months after the move, there came a day that took me off guard – a day where God stepped in and answered those prayers in an unexpected way.

This day started like all the rest – dry and hot – but I was focused on an errand I had to complete, so off I went. *I need just the right stamps.*

Celebrating the birth of my first grandchild only came once, so it was worth the extra travel to get the stamps for invitations. Pulling up to the *second* post office an odd thought jumped into my head. *Brown-eyed people. What? I haven't thought of those words for years.* I sat quietly considering them.

Years ago, those same words had made an impact on my heart – something I felt that God was saying at the time, but not knowing what it meant. Knowing this was again God today, and not my own thoughts, I sat and listened. After a couple of minutes of sitting in my car, nothing else came to mind so I continued inside to complete my errand.

I found the stamps and went up to purchase them. Without even thinking of the question before it blurted out of my mouth, I asked, "Do you have any openings or need any help covering vacations?"

To my surprise, the Postmaster excitedly responded, "Yes! And I would be happy to help with the application process and to answer any questions."

Little did I know, that day was a turning point that would lead to my answered prayer. And before I knew it, I had passed the interview and all the testing, and was an official postal employee.

During the next seven years I helped in all aspects of the post office and, to my surprise, ended up as manager of our little part-time local office. The loneliness and desire to fit in and find friends began to change as I realized God's two-word nudge: "brown-eyed people."

Those two words were His direction of a call to love – words that He had spoken to my heart so many years before.

Day in and day out I spent time with several different cultures that resided here in the dry, dusty desert – cultures of people all with beautiful brown eyes. His love for His people was revealed to me in a new way and at a new depth by my willingness to step out of my comfort zone, and into a place He had planned to use me from the beginning of time – a place where my purpose would be fulfilled by loving others into the arms of Jesus.

I am so thankful that Jesus revealed His heart to me, for all people. His love and compassion work through me daily as I do as He has directed.

My prayer to fit in and find friends had been quietly answered as He filled my life with amazing new friends, most of who were "brown-eyed people." I never knew that moving to the desert would produce a fruitful flourishing oasis in and around me.

Now our little post office is known as a place for prayer, a place to find an encouraging word, and a place where a listening ear can always be found - and, of course, a place to find just the right stamps.

Faith

Mark 9:23 - "All things are possible for one who believes."

"This isn't about 'easy belief-ism'. This is about confidence in Christ. Spend time in his presence and your confidence will grow. As it does... so will your possibilities!"[1]

Pastor Bob Clark – Crossover Ministries – Parkland, Wa.

Oh My God You Are Really REAL

Talk to Him, Like He is Real?
By Patty Johnson

I began college a believing and confirmed Lutheran girl. I prayed and attended on-campus church services for the first couple of years. However, as I studied philosophy, psychology and history, I found myself gradually becoming more and more enamored with human intellect. My professors were excited about their subjects, and I became excited as well. I began to doubt what I had learned and believed in the Bible as truth, and started to call myself an agnostic – understanding that meant I no longer believed any "absolute truths." I elevated my own ability to reason above the faith I once held dear.

It seems to me now that this transformation resulted in my moral compass diving off into the morass of marital infidelity, as well as my experimentation with other dangerous and illegal behaviors that were outside the boundaries of my Christian upbringing. "Sigh"

However, a few years into my unbelief, a woman acquaintance from my college days became an employee at the school where I was teaching. I had admired her intellect in college and considered her to be superior to me in this regard. I was surprised when in our conversation she spoke the name of Jesus as if he were a real person with whom she had a relationship. I did NOT admire this about her, thinking I knew better. However, I liked her and we were both single now, so a friendship began.

One of the traits I admired most about her was her ability to speak clearly and decisively about what she believed. I did not believe the Bible's truth as she did at that time, but I wanted to know and be able to speak about what I did believe to be true.

This friendship resulted in my starting of a journaling search for truth – as I perceived it. It also presented a simultaneous willingness to accompany her to some gatherings of Christians. You see, she and her friends showed me a love that drew me to them despite what I called our "philosophical" differences. I found our conversations to be stimulating, and they showed zero rejection of me for my unbelief.

Because of my attraction to them and their certainty of mind, I began to want to believe. I opened the Bible on numerous occasions, but when I came to supernatural happenings, I just had to close the book because I could not believe these things.

At the same time, my lengthy journaling in an attempt to reason and write out what I knew to be true had gotten me nowhere. It was as if I had picked up one end of a spool of thread as I wrote, but as I attempted to follow it to clarity of truth, I had compiled only a daunting mass of tangled thread. "Ugh!" Additionally, I had dipped into reading a bit of Eastern religious literature and became frightened as I opened that spiritual door just a crack.

Perhaps, I threw that book on top of the already-tangled mass of intellectual attempt to discern truth and walked away.

Then on one Saturday morning, around that same time frame, I attended a restaurant breakfast meeting with my Christian friend from college. After listening to the speaker's talk, I responded to his question about faith by raising my hand as someone who was interested in believing Christ. However, I did not go forward to get help with this after the meeting.

I melted into the crowd. But, in time, the gentleman approached me and asked whether I wanted to know Christ. I told him then that I had tried to read the Bible but could not believe it. He asked me, "Have you asked God for help with that?" I replied, "Do you mean talk to him like he is real?" He quickly indicated that was indeed what he meant, and suggested we pray right then and there.

I knew he meant for me to speak "out loud" to God. I was very nervous, but I closed my eyes and bowed my head with him.

He just waited for me to speak, so after a few awkward moments, I said something like, "God, help me". I didn't say anything more than those few words, but tears filled my eyes and something happened that signaled to everyone nearby, and most definitely to me that my request had been granted. Some spiritual event had taken place in me, enabling me to suddenly believe. The group gathered around to pray for me and to ask God to fill me with His Spirit. He did just that, for a joy and celebratory spirit came over me that is to this day, unparalleled in life as I know it.

Wonderful as the experience that morning was, the proof of the reality of it all came when I was home alone and opened the Bible. I found that I believed every word I read. I was stunned by the contrast to my previous attempt to read. I picked up a pen and began to underline the words that struck me as marvelously true.

My Bible became filled with underlining over the years and I have never been the same. Furthermore, I do not recall even one lapse into unbelief over the fifty-three years that have ensued since that day.

A very real God responded in the miraculous gift of faith to a very real appeal for help from one very real young woman as I talked to Him like He was real for the first time.

THANKS BE TO GOD!

A Surprise Passenger
By Linda Handschue

I was prepared for the wait as my husband entered the operating room for a 2-hour back surgery. It was just enough time to accomplish a few errands, but I never expected to find God riding along with me.

As they were prepping him for surgery, the assistant approached and asked, "Could you come with me? The doctor would like to talk with you before surgery." I didn't respond as I followed, assuming this was routine procedure. I soon found out differently.

As I sat before the doctor, he explained, "During our preparation for surgery today, I found a large spot on your husband's lung. I haven't told him and would like to wait until surgery is complete. I wanted you to be aware that this is a concern and that it could affect the outcome of today's surgery."

He then quickly rose and proceeded to the operating room to begin surgery, leaving me to process his statement – a numbness settling over me and my mind swirling as if the earth under my feet had just turned to quicksand.

Dazed, I headed out to accomplish my errands. Anxiety and fear sent a tirade of thoughts whirling through my mind. Tears were running down my face as I drove down the road. I called out to God, "Please heal my husband or, at best, have him be OK!" At that very moment I heard a voice, as clear as if someone were sitting beside me, "He will be fine...it is a scar from his childhood." Stunned, I pulled to the side of the road to process this event. Just as quickly as those words had settled over me, all the fear and anxiety flew out the window. A warm peace covered me as if I was being wrapped in a soft blanket. I knew in an instant that I had heard God speak – He had heard my prayer. Filled with what only could be explained as God's peace, I now knew my husband was going to be OK.

Returning to the hospital 2 hours later, I proceeded to the recovery room.

Surgery had gone well, my husband was alert, and I began telling him what the doctor had told me about his lung. I then told him about what happened to me in the car and about my now-unwavering faith that he was going to be fine. Just as our conversation was complete, his doctor came in to check on his progress.

Looking at us he said, "Oh, and the spot on your lung is nothing to worry about. It is old and is probably left over from your childhood." The room filled with a heavy silence as the confirmation of God's words spoken to me just a few short hours before, became reality.

God had accompanied me on my errand run – speaking and sitting right next to me, in the passenger seat of my car, pouring out a peace that surpasses all understanding. That day forever cemented my faith in a REAL God who hears and answers my prayers

Faith is All You Have
By Zelda Croskey

If ever I needed the Lord's help, I need it now. I found myself heading back to the United States, after two military tours in Germany and one in Virginia, but this was my first time traveling alone. I was returning as a single mother of three children, separated and moving toward divorce. Even though my marriage was ending, my biggest concern was *how am I going to make it?* With no job, nowhere to live, and only five hundred dollars a friend had given me, I was embarking on a journey of faith that would ultimately solidify my faith in Jehovah-jireh – My God who provides. Even my furniture and personal possessions were not coming with me, as they would be shipped to me sometime in the future. *But one thing I knew was that I had to trust God - I knew He was all I had.*

The weather was cold and the holiday season was approaching. My priority was finding a job, and my concern grew as I watched every dollar that I spent.

My children had no winter gear, so when the snow began falling I had to get them winter boots. I headed by bus to K-Mart, carefully peeling off as few bills for my purchase as possible.

My sister allowed us to stay with her and her children while I looked for work, but this arrangement was not easy. There was constant tension and we all felt unwelcome. I was in an unhappy situation here with no way out. I needed a job desperately, but everywhere I went required computer experience – and I did not have any.

Christmas was right around the corner, which brought more concern daily. Getting up early every day, I found myself walking – looking for a job, and an apartment – hoping and praying to find both. I would walk and cry out to my Heavenly Father for His help.

My faith in the Lord was strong, and I trusted him to bring me through. Little did I know that I was a candidate for a miracle – God was about to show up on my behalf.

As I prayed and believed God for provision, the doors began to open. I willingly walked through one door after another. A part-time job with Catholic Services providing home care was the first.

I knew this was not long-term and would never be enough to support us, but it would get us out of my sister's and into a place of our own.

Door two was about to fling open as I was out walking one day with my sons. We came across a nice house for rent, and peeking in the windows we saw just how nice it was. I immediately began to pray. *This is my house!* I put God on the spot – I was his daughter, I knew he would answer me and I moved out in faith. I got the number off the flyer, called the owner, met with her, and filled out the application – all while believing that this was one more "open door" that God was going to fling open.

As I sat with the owner she began to question some things, as she read out-loud from my application. At that very same moment I distinctly heard the voice of the Holy Spirit speak "Don't say a word". I held my peace and watched as the Holy Spirit gently compelled her to rent the house to me with no more questions.

Before I knew it, we were moving into a nice two-story home for just $630 a month, and all before Christmas. We began the move-in process with blankets and a borrowed 15-inch television set.

Just sleeping on the floor in our own place had us rejoicing.

But God wasn't done with his blessings. Unbeknownst to me, a wonderful sister in Christ turned in my family's name to be a recipient of a Christmas blessing.

The phone rang, and the woman on the other end began to inquire whether I was ready for Christmas. She wanted to know if I had a tree or if I had done any Christmas shopping; which, with a heavy heart, I sadly answered no about both. By the end of the call, she knew my children's ages, what toys and games they liked, and even what I might want for Christmas (though my main concern was not for me, but for the happiness of my children). She listened, and then told me she would be in contact with me again soon. I knew this was Father God letting me know – yet again – He was watching over me and my children. He was pouring out abundance beyond just "needs," and was extending it to our Christmas.

About two weeks before Christmas, a pickup truck pulled up in front of the house to deliver a large, beautiful Christmas tree – the biggest one I'd ever had – plus all new decorations!

There were four beautifully-wrapped presents for each of my children along with envelopes with $10 in spending money. And they didn't forget me – I also got a couple of presents along with two envelopes, each containing a $50 gift certificate to a local grocery store! And as if that wasn't already enough of a blessing, there was also a huge box filled with bulk food items. That was definitely God doing abundantly more than we could ask or even think!

My faith was growing leaps and bounds. Though it was still a scary time for us, I set my heart to trust God continually. I knew I would survive and that I could move forward for my children's sake.

At the beginning of the year I enrolled in a short program that included a course for beginners in computer technology. Along with computer skills they included office skills and other refresher courses such as English. I did so well that I was voted class president. God was giving me such favor. At the end of the program, a major company sent representatives to choose one person to hire into an entry-level position.

Seven of us interviewed that day; God's hand of divine favor prevailed on my behalf with the manager that interviewed me, and I got the job.

I worked for that company for 11 years, which allowed me to buy my own nice home with 4 bedrooms - giving us all plenty of room. It provided for me and my children all the way through graduation.

One of the greatest challenges of my life was raising my children alone and keeping them protected and safe. I got through it by faith; I stayed before the Lord, I prayed and prayed, and I trusted Him. My children were not my friends; they were my children who God entrusted to me. He brought us through, just as he continues to do right now – moment by moment.

If ever you find yourself alone or if life throws that curve ball, know that God is faithful, true to His word, and He loves you! He will never leave you nor forsake you.

True Stories of When God Shows Up

Wisdom

Proverbs 21:30 - No wisdom, no understanding, no counsel can avail against the LORD.

"Your enemies disappear when God whispers in your ear. Obstacles melt. Strategies of Satan disappear. The road ahead is clear when you listen to the wisdom of God."[1]

Pastor Bob Clark – Crossover Ministries – Parkland, Wa

Oh My God You Are Really REAL

"Here am I, Send me!"
By Veronica Erickson

The phone was ringing from the coast of Washington, across the ocean to Romania, as I waited to hear Mom's voice. Our Saturday morning calls were like clockwork, but on this day our pleasant conversation was not to be; I found her very overwhelmed and upset.

My Mom and her husband, Andy, had celebrated their birthdays last month: his 90th and her 75th. Everything seemed to be fine, but Andy's health had taken a rapid downward turn since then. Despondently, Mom explained that a recent diagnosis of Dementia and Alzheimer's had been made, and that her husband was quickly changing. Andy was becoming aggressive, and she was feeling helpless and frightened.

I listened as she poured out her concerns, doing the best to encourage her, all the while knowing the distance between us left me unable to help.

I hung up the phone with a heavy heart and a prayer for God's direction.

At church the next morning, as I sat listening to the message, I heard the voice of the Lord say, "Whom shall I send?" Without any hesitation, I answered, "Here am I, Send me," though I didn't yet know what this meant. I arrived home and could not let go of the whispered voice of God inside of me, and I started weeping. It was in that moment that I realized I had to go to Romania to help my Mom. I shared this with my husband, and he agreed with me; we both knew I needed to leave on my journey as soon as possible. By the end of the day I had a one-way plane ticket to Romania, not knowing when I would come back home to my own family.

Monday morning arrived and I faced the reality of the last hurdle before my journey: notifying my employer of my plans. I explained my need to leave the country on such short notice and that I didn't know when I would return. His response, "Do what you need to do, just keep me posted," brought a huge sigh of relief.

On the outside, I was frightened and overwhelmed, but inside my heart I knew I was doing the right thing. I knew the peace of God in a very real way. So, in less than a week, I walked off a plane on the other side of the world, not knowing what the next day would bring.

Andy's illness was progressing rapidly; in just a week he had fallen and injured his hip, was immobile, angry, and confused most of the time. Mom realized she could not provide the necessary care for him in her small apartment, and felt placing Andy in a nursing home would be the best for both of them.

I was supportive of my Mom's conclusion. However, the Romanian culture does not embrace this kind of decision easily; my sister, who also lives in Romania, would not hear of such a possibility. Andy's daughter, who lives in Germany, was simply in denial about her dad's health and couldn't believe this was happening to her Dad. So here we were, three siblings with three different opinions, trying to communicate, discuss, and deal with two elders who had their own frustrations.

This situation was extremely challenging as I carried pain and concern for Mom, compassion for Andy, and frustration with a sister who refused to help. Each day found myself stepping into different aspects of the process, such as filling out applications for financial aid, researching and even visiting different homes. I was thankful for my knowledge of the language, but after having been gone for over 30 years, everything had changed! There were so many challenges, and I was very overwhelmed.

With every step I took, I'd call out to the Lord to walk me through it. And time after time He provided direction, help and positive encouragement. God's direction was so obvious that Mom was amazed, and one day remarked, "Everywhere you go, the doors open for you." I knew it was not me – it was His wisdom and love.

A doctor arrived at the home to examine Andy for a second opinion on his status. He did not say anything new regarding Andy's health, but the doctor did point out one thing that made our current decision-making process even more imperative.

"This situation is more serious for your mother. If something isn't done to help her, you could potentially lose her before you lose him." My Mom had a heart condition, and the doctor was telling us this situation had become critically stressful on her heart. But even this didn't change my sister's mind. She was 100% against the use of a nursing home, and her approach to the situation continued to upset Mom. I wondered, "What would it take to change my sister's mind?"

I felt discouraged and hopeless, and I was very upset with my sister. After the doctor left, I desperately needed encouragement and a listening ear, so I picked up the phone and dialed my girlfriend who lived close by – right there in Bucharest.

But the voice on the other end of the phone was not my girlfriend – it was my pastor – in the United States! I dialed a local call – not an international call – but God made the connection. I will never have an explanation or know how this could have possibly happened, but I do know that I serve a God that cares and pays attention to every detail in my life.

He knew in that moment that I needed a word of encouragement and someone to pray for me, and that my pastor was the right person for what I needed in the moment.

It looked as if Mom and I were on our own, but after much prayer I encouraged her to move forward with her decision.

I was told about a facility in the same district my Mom lived in, so I visited, talked to the director, and began the paperwork. We were pleased with the idea that we finally found something that was close by, clean and affordable. Unfortunately, our pleasure was short-lived when we were told it could take up to three months for everything to be approved. "Three months before Andy can be taken there? This just won't work!" My heart sank as I tried to comprehend this devastating news.

Andy's condition was spiraling downhill daily and was even worse at night. He would have hallucinations, scream randomly and would want to get up and leave the room. It was very hard to keep him calm even with the medications we were giving him. It was hard to get any sleep, for at any moment his yelling might startle us.

He would be much calmer during the day, but we had work to do so there was no time for rest.

After three weeks of physical and emotional exhaustion, a phone call came from Andy's daughter.

To my amazement, she said, "I found a nursing home online. It looks good and is affordable. Would you please go and check it out?" She was in agreement with us for the first time and was even willing to help financially. Two days later we were able to move Andy into the nursing home.

When I left the United States in the middle of November, I did not know how long I would be gone. Thankfully I was able to return in just over a month and be home with my own family for Christmas – what a gift from God!

I learned a lot from that experience in Romania – lessons that will always stay with me.

I now have confidence to approach God and know that if I ask, He hears and He answers – often in ways we least expect. God is the conductor, and if I keep my eyes on Him and follow His direction, He will orchestrate the perfect symphony.

I learned that none of us know what today, tomorrow or next month will hold, and that each day is a gift from God. Those things we think we will do tomorrow may never come. We can make our plans, but the LORD determines our steps. It is His wisdom and direction that opens doors and allows for our tomorrows. Our job is to listen and obey, and say, "Here am I, Send me!"

Road-trip of Rain and Revelations
By Makalai Michaels

My brain began to shift from REM sleep to that moment just before you open your eyes, when it dawned on me: *today is the day.* I opened my eyes and began to reflect on all the things I had to do to prepare for this day. The anticipation woke me before my alarm commanded me to, which meant I had a whole hour to gather myself before my feet hit the pavement. I headed for the bathroom and suddenly I heard the voice of the Lord, very quiet and gentle, ask me a question.

"Did you confirm your hearing?" the Lord said.

"What?" I responded with confusion.

"Did you confirm your hearing?" he repeated.

The question hung in the air like a wet blanket and then one by one the words began to drop like bombs from the sky: *Did. You. Confirm. Your. Hearing.*

Suddenly I could hear the voice of the woman at the courthouse, "On page four of your motion it says you must call by the Wednesday before your hearing to confirm you still want to have your motion heard before the judge. Otherwise we will drop your case and you'll have to start over."

Shock and amazement began to flood my emotions as I said aloud, "I forgot to confirm my hearing." Immediately my mental list of things to do was thrown into chaos. An out-loud tirade spilled from my mouth, "This is going to set me back another month. This is going to cost me another $300. I have to remake copies of everything. I'm going to miss another day of class. My professors are going to think I'm lazy for missing so many days. I'll have to get a babysitter for another day." As the seconds turned to minutes my thoughts went further and further.

Finally, I said, mostly to myself, "Oh God, what am I supposed to do?" I wasn't particularly talking to the Lord, but he answered anyway. "Go to Spokane."

At this moment of frustration my brother called, sensing the irritation in my voice, he asked with concern, "What's wrong, Sis?" I was angry and began to tell him how stupid I was.

"Well," I began, "I was supposed to go to Spokane for court today to have the first of three hearings to get my felony record vacated. A month ago, I went out there getting papers signed and spent the entire day running back and forth – literally, the offices were a block apart from each other. I started at the courthouse, but was told to go to the Prosecuting Attorney's office. They signed my paper, but I had to return to the courthouse to make four sets of copies. Then I had to take the copies back to the Prosecuting Attorney's office to get an original stamp on each copy. After which I had to take the papers to the scheduler so she could give me a court date. However, the scheduler told me I didn't have to come to her to pick a date, I could just pick a date 14 days out. Once the day was picked I had to take it *back* to the Prosecuting Attorney's office so they could add me to their calendar, and then take the motion back to the scheduler and finally file the paper with the county clerk." I breathlessly ended by telling him I was just not excited to go through that entire process again.

"Don't go then, just wait till Monday," He replied to my rambling.

"I have to go," I began again, "Every day counts. Plus, I don't want to have this hanging over my head all weekend."

"What about just sending it through the mail?" he suggested.

"No that will take too long and people won't have the same sense of urgency as they would if I was standing in their office looking them in the eye. No, I'll drive!"

"Ok. Well, be safe and call me later." he said as we ended our call.

It was still early but time was not on my side. I needed to get my son up and ready for school – which took an entire hour – sending me further behind my time schedule. Then, adding to my lack of time, my phone rang again and it was my sister in Christ with encouraging words for my hearing. I cut her short and told her that there will be no hearing because, like an idiot, I forgot to confirm my hearing. She listened very patiently and then said, "Go to court anyways. Look professional and show up to the courtroom like you're supposed to be there, and don't say anything about not confirming."

"Ok, I will," I said.

We exchanged a few more words as I grabbed a change of clothes for court. Finally, by 10:30 I had my son to school (late), my car picked up (late), but was on the road headed to court. Looking at my music playlist and considering the events of the morning, I decided it was a worship kind of ride – a definite plus for the 4.5 hours ahead.

Unfortunately, the craziness of my morning was not yet over, still 90 minutes from my destination I was pulled over and ticketed for speeding, in my vain attempt to make up the hour I had lost due to all the chaos.

After passing through the mountains, you notice how flat the land is in Eastern Washington and you can see for miles in almost any direction. I noticed the layout of the clouds – to my right and left it was sunny and bright, but directly in front of me was an area of heavy, dark clouds that were very intimidating. I said aloud, "Lord, I don't want to go there. Can you please make the road turn so I don't end up there in that dark spot?" Soon the road turned and the darkness was to my right and I was headed towards sunny skies.

I praised the Lord for answering my prayer, but 20 minutes later the road turned and I was once again heading into the darkness. This time I accepted my fate.

The Lord revealed to me that the interpretation I had of the darkness had to do with my feelings about the city of Spokane in general – not the fact that it was experiencing heavy rain.

The hours and miles passed quickly as music filled the car, and in my head, I heard the Lord whisper, "Are we going to talk about this?"

I turned the music down as I realized I had been trying to drown out the voices; the lies the enemy was shouting at me as well as the truths the Lord was whispering. I decided to inquire of the Lord asking aloud "Lord, what am I going to do about this situation? I don't have time or money to deal with this extra hearing. This is my final quarter and I'm missing so many days of class to deal with this." He said nothing. I continued, "Lord, to be honest, I am having a crisis of faith right now. Sometimes I don't feel as though you are moving in my life."

"It's hard for me to separate what has happened as a result of my footwork and what has happened because you made it happen." My conversation with the Lord continued, "I feel like I'm doing a lot of work right now and I'm being rewarded for that work, but I also feel like I'm praying and nothing is happening." Again, He said nothing.

I passed a freeway sign stating "Spokane 33 miles", just as <u>Rain on Us</u> by Earnest Pugh came softly through the speakers, raindrops began to hit my windshield and they matched the energy of the song. I was mesmerized. The song speaks of the Holy Spirit raining down on us and breathing new life into us. *Ok Lord, you have my attention,* I thought.

For the next 30 minutes, the music coming out of my speakers spoke directly to my heart; <u>Oceans</u> by Hillsong played, speaking of the Lord taking us to a deeper place. As I pulled up to the courthouse <u>I Trust You</u> by James Fortune & Fiya completed the serenade, confirming to trust in the Lord even when I didn't know or understand what was going on.

Despite my chaotic morning and speeding ticket, I managed to make good time and arrived at the courthouse with time to change my clothes.

I did a final paperwork check and headed into the courthouse – like I belonged there. Not knowing which courtroom, I was to be in, I headed to the clerk's office.

I walked into the office with confidence and said, "I'm supposed to have a hearing today but I can't find my name." She searched and of course couldn't find my name either.

"What is your hearing about ma'am?" She asked patiently.

"I'm here to have my interest removed from my Legal Financial Obligations so I can have my felony vacated." I respond matter-of-factly. She didn't ask me if I confirmed my hearing and I didn't offer that detail. She turned and asked a coworker where those hearings are usually held then repeated the directions back to me.

Standing with the group congregated at the door of the courtroom, I walked up to a woman holding a stack of papers. After she finished with the other group of people, she turned and asked my name. As she began the search of her pile, I thought to myself, *She is not going to find my paper because I didn't confirm my hearing.*

Then, with the last page of her huge pile in hand she said, "Oh, here you are. Since you paid the principal of $1,500 in full, the Prosecuting Attorney agreed and the Judge signed off to waive your $1,225 in interest charges. Here is your copy of the order."

My heart stopped. I was in shock, awe and joy all at the same time. My brain forced my mouth to speak, "Thank you." I asked the next steps and was told to come by the office on Monday to talk to the person who would input and confirm how long before I could schedule my next hearing.

"I just drove 4 hours to get here and have to drive 4 hours to get home – can I just call her?" I asked.

"Sure, let me get her number. You know you could have called this morning and we would have let you know the agreement was already made. We could have faxed you the signed motion."

"It's okay. I needed this drive," I reply with a smile.

As I turned to leave I decided to take the stairs, with wobbly legs of joy and shock. A replay of the day began to run through my mind, as I took one step at a time. I began to see what God had set up for me. I still chose to walk in obedience though I could not see.

I thanked Him for the small voice that had questioned whether I had confirmed my hearing. If the Lord had not asked me that question, I would have thought what happened was a result of my footwork, and not the grace, mercy and favor of the Lord. Tears of joy and repentance flooded my eyes and streamed down my face blinding me, as I prayed for the Lord to guide my feet so I wouldn't fall down the remaining steps.

Once on the bottom floor I burst through the front doors, grateful for the rain. I had parked my car directly across the street and as I approached it the Lord told me I had been in such a hurry when I arrived that I hadn't paid for my parking. But not to worry: the spot I had taken had plenty of time left on the meter.

I cried harder as I got into my car.

I now knew that the Lord had indeed heard every prayer, worked out all the details for the day to keep me covered, and was not disappointed by my confession of doubt. And He now filled me with His unending love.

Gathering my wits, I returned a call to the sister in Christ who had called me earlier.

When she answered on the second ring I immediately sang, "My God is great, so mighty and strong, there is nothing my God cannot do for me!" I began to sob uncontrollably as I told her how God had orchestrated my day. She cried, prayed and praised the Lord with me.

I was soon back on the road for my 4-hour journey home, only now with the atmosphere in the car completely different. It was full of joy and amazement.

I rejoiced at how deeply the Lord loves me, and how even in the small details of life He cares, He speaks, He directs. His wisdom overshadows the dark clouds and above all His love is faithful, true and unending.

Nail-Polish Wisdom
By Marilyn Love

I suddenly sat up in bed from a dead sleep – *I didn't lock my car!* Spending the night at my friend's house, who lived in a high-crime area I really didn't want to chance it. So, at 2:00am - I quickly dressed and glanced out the window noticing the snow was really coming down. As I carefully stepped out onto the slippery sidewalk, my trendy new bellbottom pants left a strange pattern behind me and made an awkward swish-swish sound atop the mounting snow. It almost made me laugh – I had just flown back from sunny L.A., the only place to find pants like these – and they weren't exactly practical for deep snow.

I slowly maneuvered my way across the snowy sidewalk, and when I had almost reached my car, a police car pulled up alongside me.

Rolling down his window, the officer asked if I'd seen a man and a woman run through the area in the last few minutes. The freshly-fallen snow showed there were no footprints except mine, and I smiled as I shared my observation with him.

His partner opened the backdoor of the car and in a deep, raspy voice said, "Get in." I turned down his offer because I was so close to reaching my car. I explain about the need to lock my car when he asked what I was doing outside at this time of night. He then demanded, "Get in now!" So, I complied thinking they just wanted to help get me to my car safely in this dangerous area. Unfortunately, nothing was further from the truth!

The doors automatically locked as the car pulled away from the curb. I quickly became concerned as we began driving away from my car and instead headed towards the busy cruising road called "The Ave."

Just as I realized the inside lights were on and that the passing cars could see me sitting in the back of the cop car, a group of my friends drove by.

I watched as I saw them gawking and rubbernecking to make sure they are seeing correctly.

I wanted to yell, *I only went out to lock my car!* The look of disbelief on their faces reflected their unspoken discussion, "That can't be Marilyn. She's the last person who would be in the back of a cop car!" As I was trying to think of how I would overcome this humiliation, I saw my store manager drive by – staring at me with wide eyes and jaw hitting the floor.

I found my voice and timidly asked where we were headed, and got a curt response, "We're headed to the crime scene." For the first time, I began hearing that I was a solid suspect in an armed robbery that had just occurred.

"What? Isn't that holding up a place with a gun?" I questioned, nearly scoffing – I'd never even touched a gun and this was clearly just a ridiculous mistake! But any bit of confidence I thought I had, went out the window like a vapor when the cop answered, "*You ought to know, sister!*"

My head started spinning. *Wait, wait, wait – this just doesn't make sense! This can't really be happening! I was only walking out to lock my car, and now I'm in the back of a police car being treated like a criminal!*

Then my "fix it" mindset kicked in and I decided I needed some FACTS. I asked for a full description of the female suspect, and the response slammed me right between the eyes: A young female, approximately 20 to 24 years of age, Italian or Spanish decent, waist-long dark brown hair, white turtleneck sweater, and a brown suede jacket. *Oh my gosh. That's me to a T!* My brain was now on speed dial for more information, "Wait! What kind of pants did she have on?" I asked the officer as the radio instantly responded: herring-bone bell bottom pants. Shock overwhelmed me. I bought my cool pants knowing nobody here would have them yet, and now these unique pants were sinking my ship. I fit the description perfectly – if I didn't know me, I'd think I was the robber.

The police car pulled up to a tavern on 6th Avenue, and the cops asked me to get out. I did as I was requested and followed them, passing several people who stared at me. Then just as quickly as we had gotten out of the car, we were then heading back to it. Directing me to slide back into the seat, the cop declared, "Well, case closed. We're taking you down to the jail and booking you for armed robbery."

"Wait!" I screamed, "Who said I was guilty? Where are my accusers?" His partner informed me that the people we had just walked passed, including an off-duty police officer, had all positively identified me as the woman who held a gun to the bartender's head. My heart sunk.

"God, help me. I need wisdom and I need it now." I tearfully whispered. Then, in a flash, new thoughts began pouring into my head. I felt like I was on fire with renewed energy, my brain was running faster than a speeding bullet, peace filled my heart, and instantly my mouth was ready to speak.

The next thing I heard was my voice saying, "Ok officers, if these two citizens are able to identify me right here, right now, I want them to sign a legally-binding statement of what my hands look like. Are my hands big or small? Do I have any scars they can describe? What color of fingernail polish do I have on?" These questions had to be coming from God, not me, because I had never worn fingernail polish. In fact, I chewed my nails so badly that I'd been ashamed of them for the last 20 years!

After obtaining the requested information, the policeman came back to the car and read their statements, both of which described the female robber as wearing a pearl white nail polish. I dangled my ugly, stubby, bitten, unpolished nails in front of those two cops while tears of joy ran down my face. The shock on their faces was priceless.

The drive back to my car was pretty quiet – all their "hot air" had been expelled as these cops processed this quick turn of events.

How would I have thought fingernail polish (or lack of) would change the outcome of this case! My 60-minute nightmare was finally over and I was about to get some much-needed sleep – but I would always remember this night as one where my thoughts were not my own, but instead the wisdom and direction of my God as he responded to my humble prayers and faith.

God had shown himself real to me and pulled me right out of the fire just like He had for Shadrach, Meshach, and Abednego in the Bible.

What did you think of *Oh My God You Are Really Real*?

Thank you for purchasing this book. I know you could have picked any number of books to read, but you picked this one and for that I am extremely grateful.

I hope that it added value and quality to your everyday life – encouraging and inspiring you to see every life event as a possible encounter with a very REAL God. If so, it would be very appreciated if you could post a review on Amazon.

In this age of publishing, every review is critical to the success or failure of any book. Your honest feed-back will make a difference.

Thank you again, for taking the time to read this book.

Contributing Authors, Editors and Artists

J. K. Sanchez – Author, Graphic Design and Publisher

J.K. grew up in Las Vegas - fleeing the heat - she and her husband escaped to the Pacific Northwest 3+ decades ago. Her savored moments are those spent with her husband – the love of her life, as well as her children and grandchildren. Two dachshunds at her feet keep her days active as she spends her retired time saturated in her passions for photography, growing flowers and of course writing.

As an author and photographer J.K.'s love for people and nature is portrayed both through visually descriptive prose (devotional studies in Nature vs Spiritual, non-fiction short stories and essays) as well as through the eye of the camera. Her spiritual passion for worship and the presence of the Lord draws her continually to see freedom proclaimed and released to others through the finished work on the cross of Jesus.

Oh My God You Are Really REAL

As an author, her books include: a 4 book devotional series (Winters Rest (2014), Spring's Assurance (2015), Summer's Delight (2015), Fall's Yield (2015)) Inspirational collection (Reflection of His Glory (2015)), Multiple journals and a Prayer Journal (Access to the Throne (2017)) as well as contributor to (Keeper of the Faith (2016). As a photographer she has participated throughout Washington in gallery events and fairs, has photographed weddings, memorials, children, pets and personal portraits, currently has a published CD of her graphic landscape photographs (Names of God (2016)) as well as contribution of photographs for (Keeper of the Faith (2016)).

Her books are available on amazon.com as well as J.K.Sanchez.com
She is also available at facebook.com/authorJKSanchez
facebook.com/majesticreflections
facebook.com/JudyKSanchezPhotography
And don't miss her current blog at
unearthinghistreasures.wordpress.com
Email: jksanchez.author@gmail.com

Kasey Zeigler - Author

Kasey was born in upstate New York. She honorably served her country active duty in the Air Force for 12 years and then went on to work 26 years civil service, while also serving another 10 years in the Air Force Reserve. She earned a Business Administrative degree through several colleges while on active duty. While in the military, she had the opportunity to travel to many countries and experience many cultures. Kasey is currently actively involved in her non-denominational church in Tacoma WA, and serves on the worship team. She also works in the automotive shop of her Worship Team Pastor. Her greatest love outside of Jesus, her two adult sons and her church is crochet. Many have benefited from the prayer shawls, hats and scarves that she makes and gives away.

Donna Jackson – Author & Editor

Raised and living in Las Vegas, Nv.: Donna Jackson enjoys life with her husband of 38 years. Donna spent 12 years in banking but now loves spending her time with her two adult children as well as her household full of "fur babies". Her passions are rescuing pets, gardening, photography, collecting rocks and camping.

Makalai Michaels - Author

Originally from California Makalai Michaels moved to Washington in 1994 to be reunited with her family. Having lived in Washington since then she now considers herself a Pacific Northwest Native. Currently she is raising two boys as a single mother and pursuing her master's degree in nonprofit management. She works with single mothers in the area to help them reclaim their identity in Christ and move forward in the story that has been written about them. One of her favorite quotes is..."Believe in the mission that has been set before you, go forth with passion and dedication knowing that you are exactly where you are supposed to be - doing exactly what you are supposed to be doing".

Marilyn Love - Author

Marilyn Love is retired and enjoying life. She is a Life Coach; encouraging people to be all that they can be and to live their life to the fullest. She is a national speaker who has a way of capturing her audience with her wit, inspiration and practical strategy applications. You'll enjoy her writing style as she tells her story all the while drawing you into it.

Bonnie Simmons - Author

Bonnie Simmons is a wife to her best friend Dean, mother to 3 amazing kids: Austin, Zoe & Autumn, and 1 teenage puppy Angus. She and her husband are associate pastors and business owners. Her hobbies include camping, cooking, worshipping with her family and dark chocolate.

Christine Vanderhoff - Author

Born in Washington and raised in California - Christine Vanderhoff moved back to Washington as an adult desiring to launch into a new life. Her faith and love for Jesus has never wavered and she knows that no matter where she walks He is always there for her. Working as a Community Relations Assistant in a Senior Care facility she is able to share her faith and love of life with the residents and families. Christine has always loved being around seniors and has a heart for them. She shines as she actively shares the love of Christ with the families and residents. Her faith brings peace and assurance to families as they transition their family member into their new home. Faith brings a hope that only HE can provide in one's life and that's something she knows quite well in her own.

Stacy Wind - Author

Stacy Wind was born and raised in Las Vegas, Nv. She married a local headlining magician and has been his assistant for several years - having the opportunity to perform on stage and on television. Adding to that busy lifestyle Stacy is camera ready as a corporate promotional model through-out the area.

Her personal passions surround her as her home is filled with rescue cats and dogs. She has been an animal activist for many years, finding homes for even the most unwanted and sometimes rather wild "furry friends".

Dustie Verwers - Author

Living in Washington her entire life, Dustie Verwers is a true lover of the Northwest. She enjoys hiking and all things nature. She is happily married with 3 amazing adult children. Real Estate is more than a career for her and her husband; she thrives in its opportunities. As a deacon in her church – her ministry to the body of Christ in practical ways is very obvious to those she serves. Dusties greatest passion is to bring glory to the lover of her soul – Jesus!

Dennis Sanchez - Author

Creativity flows from Dennis Sanchez whenever he picks up a pencil. An artist since his teens, he enjoys multiple mediums as different styles emerge. He has painted landscapes, portraits and prophetic worship paintings throughout his life. His favorite times are spent with his wife of over 40 years, his children and grandchildren as well as his two "fur babies". He enjoys nature, the ocean, as well as feeding and watching the birds and squirrels that habitat in his own back yard. His love for the Lord stirs him with a passion for the Presence of God and to see the sick healed.

Linda Handschue – Author

Linda was born in Calif. and raised in Las Vegas, Nv. where she still resides with her husband. She is a mother of two grown sons and loves spending time with them. Family and trips to the ocean when possible are her favorite times of life! Her passion for Animal activism and environmental issues driver her interests. Although she has a busy life she will tell you God is and will always be number one. "He is always with me!"

Lorena Hartzog - Author

As a Postmaster in one of the smallest Post Offices in Washington, Lorena is a delight, as she meets the needs of customers entering her workplace. While waiting to be serviced, there is a photo gallery available for viewing over 200 current photos she has taken. She changes the gallery once a month, revealing her love for the natural beauty surrounding all who live in that area.

She has, on numerous occasions, let people know she will pray for them. This small Post Office houses many who have not had the desire to enter a church. Just knowing someone is praying for them is appreciated and sparks much more than prayer. Friends that care are all around. She is more than willing to be used by the Spirit of the Lord.

Randy Love – Author

Randy Love is a man filled with love and forgiveness. Though disabled, he finds purpose in life and lives it to the fullest. His story may surprise you as you find yourself brought into it's depth of truth. His desire is for you to recognize that power of love and forgiveness for your life.

Melissa Lee - Author

Melissa Lee was born and raised in Bellingham, WA. One of 4 girls, she and her sisters were raised in a home where Jesus Christ was center. At the age of 8 Melissa accepted Jesus Christ as her Lord and Savior, and since has dedicated her life to knowing Him more, and sharing her love for Christ through music and writing. Melissa cherishes her relationships with her family and friends, and is the PROUD Auntie of 5 amazing children who all serve Jesus Christ. She currently resides in Tacoma serving the local Church, and works in her community as a Head Start Assistant Teacher. It is her desire that as you read her story you would encounter the truth about who God truly is- the God of reconciliation and restoration.

Mark Johnson – Author

A passionate father and grandfather, Mark Johnson is a life-long gardener with a special love of cows and chickens. He is a gifted craftsman who works fulltime as a carpenter and excels in producing doors that are true works of art. He lives with his much-loved wife in Yelm, Wa. Mark is faithful in his church, loves God and enjoys reading and writing.

Patty Johnson – Author

As a semi-retired schoolteacher in Yelm, WA, Patty Johnson has enjoyed many years working with children. She loves her husband, her church, and above all her God. Praying for her family, her students, and her country has been and continues to be a passion in her life.

Zelda Croskey - Author

An ordained minister of the Gospel with a Prophetic and Intercessor calling, Zelda has been a Spirit-filled Christian for nearly four decades. Her greatest joy and fulfilling accomplishment is in being a mother, and now a grandmother. She takes joy in fulfilling God's plans and purposes for her life.

Zelda has a heart-felt call to the nations, following continually the path that the Lord sets before her. It is her life's journey to complete the call of God, and to see people delivered and set free from every sin and bondage of the enemy and to proclaim the goodness and love of God to all mankind.

Nicholas W. Smurro - Author

Born in Texas, Nicholas W. Smurro is the eldest son and fourth of seven children. As an Air Force family, by high school graduation Nick had lived in Alaska, Washington, California, Missouri, Puerto Rico, Illinois, Japan and Hawaii. Moving around afforded many adventures. Some favorites included skiing, snowboarding, mountain climbing, sailing, surfing and diving, as well as many school sports. Work opportunities were numerous; Nick has worked as a firefighter, phlebotomist, racquetball instructor, ski technician, English teacher, pizza deliverer, waiter, lawn boy and chicken catcher.

After attaining bachelor degrees in biology, chemistry and psychology and doing research at the National Institute of Health, he earned his Doctorate of Chiropractic. Soon after, he opened his Chiropractic clinic in Washington and continues to live and practice there today.

Music has always been a part of Nick's joy in life - playing trumpet, horns, harmonica, congas and multi percussion. He finds his greatest love in Jesus and thus his greatest musical passion (and expression) in playing on the worship team. A favorite nourishment of his soul comes from cruising the waters of the great northwest with his son, Nolan and dog, Cappy.

Shellia Reed – Author

Shellia Reed lives in Lakewood, Washington with various wild creatures (deer, rabbits, coyotes, raccoons) that pass through her yard upon occasion. She loves travelling and is almost always ready for a new adventure. She enjoys reading, writing, crafting, and the relatively new pass-time of painting rocks. She loves spending time with family and friends and especially enjoys time with her great nieces and great nephew. She spends some of her spare time checking items off her bucket list. (Skydiving is NOT on it!) She is a CASA (Court Appointed Special Advocate) volunteer for foster children, advocating on their behalf with the court and social service agencies. The work swings between being heartbreaking and being joyous. She prays that she's making a difference for these children, one life at a time.

Shellia was blessed to grow up in church, although her parents did not attend. Her auntie began taking her to Sunday School at age 2. She accepted Jesus as her Savior at age 6. She has found the Lord to be faithful, loving, trustworthy, merciful, gracious, glorious, lovely, and more and more precious as the years pass.

When challenged by this question, "What is the most interesting thing about you", she decided that the answer is "The fact that Shellia Reed is loved unconditionally by GOD ALMIGHTY, KING OF THE UNIVERSE'" is her most important aspect. She is eternally grateful for this truth!
Her favorite scripture is Romans 5:8
"But God demonstrates His own love toward us, in that while we were still sinners, Christ died for us."

Veronica Erickson – Author

Veronica was born and raised in Bucharest, Romania. The country was under a communist leadership during that time but with strong faith and high hopes, she left her family behind to find a new a new life in an unknown land.

She lives in Washington with her husband Duke and their son brings them much pride. Veronica has served in many different ministries at her church and the local Christian Community; she currently leads the First Impression Ministry at Zion's River Church and is a Children's Leader for Bible Study Fellowship.

Amber Sanchez – Editor & Graphic Design

Amber Sanchez is a freelance website developer who focuses on copywriting and graphic design. Her passion lies in the non-profit sector, specifically for pro-life and women-centered businesses and ministries, with achievements being recognized both locally and nationally.

Amber and her husband, Dave, raise a blended family of four children: Jaron, Tanner, Nevan and Renna. Her kids are her pride and joy, and she leans on God's direction and blessing as she faces each new stage of parenthood.
Visit Amber's website at:
www.AmberWebsiteDesign.com

Antonia Frye - Artist

Having a passion for painting since she was 12, Antonia Frye excels in her ability to visually stir your emotions in her artwork. Her life goal is to graduate and become a teacher of social studies and art – after she has had plenty of time to travel. Being born and raised in Washington, she loves all things nature; hiking and camping bring her great joy. Antonia's love for kids, as well as her great care for both the people and animals around her makes her easily approachable. Her open mindedness and non-judgmental spirit are endearing qualities that reflect a maturity way beyond her years.

Endnotes:

Introduction 1. Pastor Jim Sheen – Believing Today. Excerpt from: Morning Meditation – More Than a Story 10/24/17. www.believingtoday.com www.zionsriver.com

Provision 1. Pastor Bob Clark – Parkland, Wa. www.crossover-ministries.net

Healing 1. Pastor Bob Clark – Parkland, Wa. www.crossover-ministries.net

Trust 1. Pastor Bob Clark – Parkland, Wa. www.crossover-ministries.net

Protection 1. Pastor Bob Clark – Parkland, Wa. www.crossover-ministries.net

Forgiveness 1. Pastor Bob Clark – Parkland, Wa.
www.crossover-ministries.net

Love 1. Pastor Bob Clark – Parkland, Wa.
www.crossover-ministries.net

Faith 1. Pastor Bob Clark – Parkland, Wa.
www.crossover-ministries.net

Wisdom 1. Pastor Bob Clark – Parkland, Wa.
www.crossover-ministries.net

Oh My God You Are Really REAL

Titles available by J.K. Sanchez

Majestic Reflection Devotional Study Series:

Winters Rest

Spring's Assurance

Summer's Delight

Fall's Yield

Stand alone or companion journals:

Winters Rest Journal

Spring's Assurance Journal

Summer's Delight Journal

Fall's Yield Journal

Majestic Reflection Journal

Reflections of His Glory Journal

Additional Titles

Reflections of His Glory

Access To The Throne! – A Prayer Journal

Contact me at: JKSanchez.author@gmail.com

Jksanchez.com

Also find me on Amazon.com

www.ingramcontent.com/pod-product-compliance
Lightning Source LLC
LaVergne TN
LVHW051552070426
835507LV00021B/2540